TEARS AND TANTRUMS

What to do when babies and children cry

Aletha J. Solter, Ph.D.

Shining Star Press
Goleta, California

Cover photo by Hannah Rosenthal
Cover design by Malin Skareke

Published by Shining Star Press, P.O. Box 206. Goleta, California 93116, U.S.A. Phone & Fax: (805) 968-1868
e-mail: awarepar@sb.net
web site: http://www.sb.net/awarepar/books.htm

Publisher's Cataloging Information

Solter, Aletha Jauch
    Tears and tantrums: what to do when babies and children cry / Aletha J. Solter
    Includes bibliographical references and index.
    ISBN 0-9613073-6-6
    1. Child rearing. 2. Parenting. 3. Crying in infants. 4. Crying in children. 5. Infant psychology. 6. Child psychology. I. Title.
    Dewey Decimal Classification: 649'.1

Library of Congress Catalog Card Number: 97-61760

Printed in the United States of America

Acknowledgments

Many thanks to all those who have organized my workshops on this topic. The thought-provoking experiences and challenging questions of hundreds of parents and teachers who have attended my workshops have given me the opportunity to refine and clarify my presentation of this material. Special thanks goes to my husband, Kenneth Solter, for his careful editing of every draft of the manuscript; to my son, Nicholas Solter, for his astute feedback; to my mother, Tonia Jauch, for her patient corrections of my grammar and spelling; to my sister, Eldri Jauch, for her insights into ways of clarifying many sections; and to my friend and colleague, Dr. Mary Galbraith, for her editorial comments and valuable suggestions. I am also grateful to Dr. Thomas Gordon, founder of the Parent Effectiveness Training movement, who has inspired me and supported my work, and who wrote the foreword.

Acknowledgments

Table of Contents

List of charts

Foreword by Dr. Thomas Gordon

Readers of this pioneering book have a lot in store for them. First, they will find it easy to read and easy to learn from. They will also be impressed because the author does not offer the reader her opinions or favorite remedies. Instead, she is a scholar who is undoubtedly more familiar with the scientific research studies for early child development and crying than anyone in the world. Dr. Solter has, for many years, been learning why children cry, what happens in their bodies when they do, and what their parents and caretakers should do to help them deal constructively with their stresses.

This book will also surprise the reader. It did me. Most readers will be astonished by what Dr. Solter advocates: allowing babies to cry (while holding them) instead of trying various ways to stop them. This book will also help the reader understand children, because the author tells what goes on inside babies' bodies as well as why they behave as they do.

This book will undoubtedly give readers more confidence as parents or caregivers, because it provides them with specific skills, in particular, procedures for dealing constructively with tears and tantrums. These new skills will bring rewards that all parents value, namely, children who are healthier, both physically and psychologically. Dr. Solter cites evidence that these skills also greatly reduce tensions and stress in families, thus preventing physical and verbal abuse by parents who are so often provoked and who get angry at a child's consistent crying.

I could not help but personally relate to Dr. Solter's frequent emphasis on crying as babies' only way of *communicating* to parents that they have a *problem*. This is a key element in my own model of the parent/child relationship as described in my Parent Effectiveness Training (P.E.T.) book and courses, where I emphasize the critical importance of parents recognizing when children "own" a problem. That is precisely when parents should listen with warmth and empathy, as Dr. Solter also teaches. We both urge parents (and caretakers too) to avoid trying to come up with *their* remedies to stop the child's crying.

Instead, trust that children have inner resources for dealing with their problems.

Dr. Solter urges parents to avoid responding to a child's tears and tantrums by looking for solutions or "controls" to *stop* the crying: by feeding, rocking, singing, or inserting a pacifier in the child's mouth. In my P.E.T. model I too urge parents to keep "ownership of the problem" with the child by avoiding what I call the Communication Roadblocks. Instead, parents are taught to use Active Listening, which empowers children to find their own solutions to their problems. Dr. Solter also stresses that parents should "listen to the child and accept the crying."

Dr. Solter also shares with me the strong admonishment against *any kind* of punishment. We agree that crying and tantrums reflect a genuine need and should never be considered "misbehavior."

The author has wisely added many true-to-life examples that illustrate and further validate her beliefs and the advice she gives parents. Her readers will be helped to understand the many different reasons children cry, and what parents can do to help the situation *without* trying to stop the crying. An example is her advocacy of holding children to prevent acts of violence against younger siblings rather than using punishment, which itself would be an act of violence. I was impressed with Dr. Solter's statement that "children need the most love and attention when they act the least deserving of it."

Finally, Dr. Solter greatly enhanced the value of this book by closing it with feedback she has received from parents and teachers who have read her books or attended her successful workshops. The reader will welcome their success stories as well as their most frequent questions.

Dr. Thomas Gordon
Founder, Gordon Training International
Author of *Parent Effectiveness Training* (P.E.T.)

WARNING/DISCLAIMER

This book is an educational resource, not intended to be a substitute for psychological or medical advice or treatment. Many of the behaviors and symptoms discussed (including crying and raging) can be an indication of serious emotional or physical problems. Parents and teachers are advised to consult a competent physician whenever children display behavioral or emotional problems of any kind, or when pain or illness are suspected. Crying and raging can also be an indication that a child is suffering from severe trauma, such as abuse. Furthermore, some of the suggested methods in this book may not be appropriate under all conditions or with children suffering from certain physical or emotional problems.

The mention of specific therapies in this book is for informational purposes only and does not entail endorsement by the author. Some forms of therapy can be dangerous if carried out by improperly trained practitioners. If you are considering choosing a therapist for yourself or your child, it is recommended that you carefully review the therapist's credentials and references.

The author and publisher shall have neither liability nor responsibility to any person or entity with respect to any damage caused, or alleged to be caused, directly or indirectly by the information contained in this book.

"What soap is for the body, tears are for the soul."

Jewish proverb

PART I:
SOME FACTS ABOUT TEARS AND TANTRUMS

1. INTRODUCTION: A HUGE MISUNDERSTANDING

Children's tears and tantrums are some of the most difficult behaviors for parents to cope with. In fact, parents ask more questions about crying than about any other topic. They are often baffled when their babies wake up crying at night, when their two-year-olds throw temper tantrums, or when their four-year-olds whine all day. Parents wonder how to respond to children when they cry, and whether it is appropriate to comfort, ignore, distract, punish, "give in," or listen empathically. Some parents worry that crying means the child is immature, rejecting of the parent, manipulative, or just plain "spoiled."

I have been researching the topic of crying for the past 25 years, and have made some interesting discoveries about the role of crying in healthy development. My two previous books: *The Aware Baby* (birth to age two) and *Helping Young Children Flourish* (ages two to eight) describe an approach to parenting that I call "Aware Parenting." It combines attachment-style parenting, non-punitive discipline, and acceptance of emotional release (specifically crying). These books have been translated into several languages, and I have led workshops for parents and professionals in eight different countries. Because of the considerable interest for my innovative ideas about crying, I have compiled that information into the present book.

There has been a huge misunderstanding about the meaning and purpose of tears and tantrums. During the Middle Ages in Europe, many people thought that babies and children who cried or raged a lot were possessed by a demon or devil. The treatment was to have a priest exorcise the devil from the child.

During the 18th century, attitudes began to change. Tears and tantrums were still considered evil, but gradually the blame shifted to the parents, who were told that they had been too indulgent and had "spoiled" their children. The advice was to punish children for these "misbehaviors" or at least resist "giving in" to the child. Parenting manuals from the 18th century through much of the 20th century spoke about "breaking the will of the children" so they would become docile and obedient.

For example, the following quote is from a book published in Germany in 1748:

> As far as willfulness is concerned, this expresses itself as a natural recourse in tenderest childhood as soon as children are able to make their desire for something known by means of gestures. They see something they want but cannot have; they become angry, cry, and flail about. Or they are given something that does not please them; they fling it aside and begin to cry. These are dangerous faults that hinder their entire education and encourage undesirable qualities in children. If willfulness and wickedness are not driven out, it is impossible to give a child a good education. The moment these flaws appear in a child, it is high time to resist this evil so that it does not become ingrained through habit and the children do not become thoroughly depraved.[5]

Nowadays a surprising number of books for parents still give similar advice. Authors often list temper tantrums in chapters dealing with "misbehaviors" such as hitting, biting, lying, and stealing, and advise parents to ignore or punish these outbursts. At best, parents and teachers are advised to help children express their wants and feelings using words rather than tears and tantrums, which are considered to be immature and unacceptable. Babies are still accused of "manipulating" their parents by crying. Many psychologists and doctors still advise parents to ignore their babies' cries in order to break this habit and to teach babies to soothe themselves.

At the other extreme is the more recent "back-to-nature" movement that recommends responding to every cry with a nurturing, soothing response (such as nursing or rocking), to quiet down the baby. Advocates of this approach are justifiably reacting against centuries of harmful advice. However, this approach, loving as it may appear to be, still fails to recognize an important function of crying. Furthermore, it places an impossible burden on parents by making them believe that their job is to stop babies and children from crying.

This book proposes an entirely new way of thinking about crying and raging, representing a breakthrough in understanding children's needs and emotions. It is best if babies and children who cry are never ignored. Their cries should always receive a nurturing response.

However, *not all crying is an indication of an immediate need or want.* Much of it is a natural stress-release mechanism that allows children to heal from the effects of frightening or frustrating experiences that have occurred previously. Children use tears and tantrums to resolve trauma and release tensions. It is therefore not the caretaker's job to stop the crying or raging, because these behaviors are, in themselves, basic needs from birth on.

An understanding of the healing effects of tears and tantrums can have beneficial consequences. In addition to helping children resolve trauma and release stress, an acceptance of crying and raging can play a crucial role in preventing discipline problems and reducing hyperactivity as well as harmful behavior towards others (violence). Crying can also contribute to better physical and emotional health, attention span, and ability to learn. An added benefit of this approach is that it can help resolve sleep problems (without ignoring the child). Finally, supportive listening of children when they need to cry helps to strengthen the adult/child relationship.

My goal in writing this book is to help parents and others involved with young children to understand and correctly interpret children's crying and raging, and to respond in ways that best promote optimal development. I discuss the sources of stress that cause a need for crying, the ways in which adults typically repress crying in children, and I suggest nurturing approaches to facilitate crying as an important form of emotional release. I have gathered information from a wide variety of sources, including psychological, biochemical, physiological, and cross-cultural studies, as well as personal experiences from parents and teachers.

Children's tears and tantrums elicit strong feelings in adults. A survey in the United States asked new mothers to describe their feelings when they were unable to quiet their crying infants. The mothers mentioned feeling exasperated, afraid, anxious, unloving, resentful, and confused. Many had low self-confidence. Some even felt extreme hostility toward their infants.[1] Similar results were found in a survey of mothers in England and Australia. In this study, 80% of mothers whose babies cried extensively mentioned feeling depressed, and 50% of them felt a strong urge to hit their babies.[2]

Not surprisingly, crying has been linked to child abuse.[3] In a survey of battered infants, *80% of the parents reported that excessive crying by their infant had triggered the abuse.*[4] After the first year, many parents continue to become very upset when their children cry or rage. This occurs especially if the reason for the crying is unclear, or if the child's outburst seems to be unjustified by the incident that triggered it. Some parents feel a strong urge to punish their children at these times.

Parents need correct information, reassurance, and constructive ways of handling their children's emotional outbursts. This will contribute greatly to a reduction in child abuse and to a more harmonious family life. Teachers and caretakers can also benefit from this information.

This book is divided into four parts. Part I gives some basic information about the stress-release function of crying and raging. It reviews the research on the physiological and psychological benefits, the uses of crying in therapy with children, and the differences in crying between men and women. It also introduces the concepts of repression and control patterns.

Part II discusses crying in infants up to one year of age, and Part III discusses crying and raging in children from one to eight years of age.

In Part IV, I describe some practical applications, emphasizing the concept of creating emotional safety for children. I also discuss the feelings triggered in adults by children's tears and tantrums, as well as steps people can take to feel more tolerant. There is a section with firsthand accounts by parents using this approach, and another section in which I answer the questions most commonly asked by parents and teachers during my workshops. The book concludes with advice for professionals who work with parents about ways of supporting parents.

I am hoping that the information in this book will help people to understand children and themselves better, thereby contributing to a happier and more peaceful world.

The main points are summarized on the following page.

SUMMARY OF MAJOR POINTS

1. All children experience some stress, no matter how loving the parents are. An important function of crying is to release stress and promote healing.

2. Adults often try to repress crying in children out of a misunderstanding of crying, and because it arouses their own unresolved stress and need to cry. This repression of crying is passed on from one generation to the next.

3. In response to an environment in which crying is not accepted, children acquire certain rigid behavior patterns to keep themselves from crying.

4. The consequences of this repression of crying include emotional and behavioral problems, failure of children to reach their full potential, and later stress-related illnesses.

5. These negative consequences can be reversed when adults learn the benefits of crying, overcome their own obstacles to feeling, and provide children with the emotional safety that is needed in order to cry and heal from the effects of stress.

2. STRESS RELEASE MECHANISMS IN CHILDREN

To understand tears and tantrums, it is necessary to know the kinds of stress children are dealing with in their lives. "Stress" is a popular word, because everybody feels stressed at times. We often forget, however, that babies and children also experience stress.

Physiologists define stress as anything that disrupts the normal balance of the body. This balance is the state of the body at rest when nothing threatening or unusual is happening. It is generally referred to as "homeostasis" (meaning, literally, "staying the same"). Stress is therefore anything that disrupts the body's homeostasis.

Stress is caused by events called "stressors," of which there are two kinds: physical and psychological. Physical stress is caused by stressors involving immediate trauma to the body, such as a broken arm or a cut finger. It can also be caused by environmental stressors such as famine.

Psychological stress (also called emotional stress) is caused by stressors such as financial problems, an argument with our spouse, or an upcoming exam. The sources of psychological stress for children are quite different from those for adults. In my workshops, I ask the participants to think of specific sources of stress for children. These are listed below. These stressors cause children to feel terrified, anxious, confused, frustrated, angry, betrayed, sad, or disappointed.

MAJOR SOURCES OF STRESS FOR INFANTS AND CHILDREN

• **Hurts by commission** (direct hurts from other people):
  Physical, sexual, verbal, or emotional abuse
  Disrespectful treatment (ex: insults, lies)
  Authoritarian discipline (including all punishment)
  Pressure to learn, perform, or compete
  Unrealistically high adult expectations
  Repression or rejection of painful emotions
  Love or attention conditional on child's behavior
  Racism, sexism

• **Hurts by omission** (unmet needs):
    Physical or emotional neglect
    Insufficient physical contact (holding)
    Delay or misinterpretation of need fulfillment
    Lack of opportunities to form attachments
    Lack of attention, empathy, or sensitive responsiveness
    Lack of stimulation
    Lack of autonomy
    Unfilled promises
    Lack of information, unanswered questions

• **Situational hurts** (indirect hurts, caused by life circumstances):
    Prenatal or birth trauma
    Illnesses, injuries, medical procedures
    Permanent loss of attachments (separation or death)
    Short separations (depends on age of child)
    Overstimulation
    Developmental frustrations & fears
    Inevitable restrictions
    Major changes (ex: new sibling, home, or school)
    Parental stress (ex: anxiety, grief, anger, illness)
    Parental disputes, separation, or divorce
    Parental alcoholism or drug abuse
    Dysfunctional family system
    Natural disasters (ex: fires, floods, earthquakes)
    Exposure to violence (through real life or the media)
    Other frightening events
    Disappointments or unexpected occurrences
    Disputes with siblings or other children

Every effort should be made to reduce stress in children's lives. This is not easy, because the sources of stress are not always immediately apparent. Some children are more sensitive than others, and a similar incident, such as a change in routine, could deeply upset one child while not affecting another child at all. Adults need to be aware of each child's thought processes, feelings, and needs, and do as much as possible to make life tolerable and understandable for children.

It is also important to remember that some stress is inevitable. You cannot protect children from life itself, and learning and growing always involve some pain and frustration. When I first became a mother, I thought that my job was to protect my son from all the bad things in the world. Although this does make sense up to a certain point, I soon discovered that this goal was unrealistic. I realized that I would quickly become exhausted if I attempted to accomplish it! My job as a mother was not necessarily to protect my children from pain, difficulties, or frustrations, but rather to help them learn to cope with the resulting emotions.

Luckily, children know very well how to overcome stress by using certain stress-release mechanisms. There are four primary ways in which children cope with stress: talking, symbolic play, laughter, and crying (including raging).

Talking

If somebody is willing to listen, children will talk about events that have upset them. Adults do this too. Everybody feels the urge to tell the story of a traumatic event, and we all need listeners. However, the younger the child, the less likely he is to use talking as a stress-release mechanism, and this method is obviously useless to an infant.

Symbolic play

Symbolic play begins around two years of age.[1] In this kind of play, children reenact scenes from real life with toys and other props. This play becomes more complex as children grow older.

Children often cope with specific traumatic events through their symbolic play. For example, if a little boy's father had a car accident and was hospitalized, this child might play with toy cars and reenact the accident in an effort to understand what happened and to assimilate the distressing event.

When a child experiences a traumatic event, it is very helpful if an attentive adult observes and listens to him, shows compassion and understanding, and acknowledges his feelings. The therapeutic value of play has been recognized for several decades. Many therapists use play therapy with children to help them resolve trauma and to work through fear, grief, and anger.[2]

Laughter

Laughter begins around five months of age. Children use laughter primarily to release fears, anxieties and embarrassment. For example, the game of "peek-a-boo" can be used therapeutically with babies to help them overcome fears of separation. The baby laughs when the adult reappears, releasing in this way tensions resulting from separation anxiety. "Peek-a-boo" is most effective after six months of age, which is when the first signs of separation anxiety usually occur.

Researchers have found that laughter is very beneficial and has a positive physiological effect on the body.[3] This important healing mechanism is usually quite well tolerated by adults, even though most people do not think of laughter as therapeutic.

Crying and raging

Crying and raging are important stress-release mechanisms that are available from birth on. When a child experiences any kind of emotional pain, the natural response is to cry. For example, if a child's favorite doll breaks, she will spontaneously cry. This crying is an important and healthy release that has beneficial physiological and psychological effects. Many people recognize this, and are able to offer love and support to a child who is crying in such a situation.

Some situations are more difficult. For example, a child has a temper tantrum because she can't have an ice cream cone, or a baby wakes up several times crying at night. Parents and teachers usually welcome help in understanding and coping with these situations, which are discussed in this book.

There is always the possibility of physical pain when a child cries. When pain is suspected, medical advice and treatment are recommended.

Crying is also a possible indication of severe stress,[4] and I strongly advise parents and teachers always to look for sources of stress in children's lives. However, crying is often considered to be an unnecessary by-product of stress, and many people have the incorrect impression that children would feel better if they would only stop crying. This is incorrect. No matter what the source of stress, *children will not feel better until they have been allowed to cry and rage as much as needed.*

There are additional ways of releasing stress, including yawning, trembling, and sweating. These are silent and less obvious stress-release mechanisms, but they are just as important as laughter or crying. Sometimes they accompany laughter or crying.

3. THE PHYSIOLOGY OF STRESS AND CRYING

There are many physiological benefits of crying. To understand these, it is important to know what happens in our bodies during stress.

The stress response

Our bodies respond to all of the various kinds of stressors in the same way, whether they are physical, such as a broken toe, or psychological, such as hearing about a friend's serious illness. This physiological reaction to stress is called the "stress response," and it serves the purpose of helping us cope with emergencies. The stress response can be life-saving in cases of immediate physical danger. Eventually, however, especially if there is chronic psychological stress, this same mechanism can have a negative effect and even make us sick.

Here is a simplified summary of how the stress response works. The hypothalamus in the brain begins by sending out alarm signals that stimulate two different systems in the body: the sympathetic nervous system and the pituitary gland.

The sympathetic nervous system helps prepare the body for action by dilating the pupils, accelerating the heartbeat, increasing the blood pressure, and diverting blood flow to the muscles and away from the digestive organs. This is commonly known as the "fight or flight" response. This nervous system communicates with various body organs by means of two chemical substances called epinephrine and norepinephrine (also known as adrenaline and noradrenaline). These substances belong to a class of chemicals called catecholamines. When you are suddenly very alarmed or very excited, you often feel a clutching sensation in your stomach. This is the effect of epinephrine (adrenaline).

The pituitary gland is also activated during stress, and this results in the production of certain hormones. First of all, the pituitary gland releases a hormone into the blood stream called ACTH (adrenocorticotropic hormone). Within minutes this hormone stimulates another gland in the body, the adrenal cortex, which releases hormones called glucocorticoids. (A synthetic form of glucocorticoids is cortisone, used medically to suppress inflammations.) These hormones affect many parts of the body, all with the goal of helping the body cope with an emergency. The main function of the glucocorticoids is the mobilization of the body's energy resources to meet the demands of stress.

Normally, increased glucocorticoid levels in the blood cause the production of ACTH by the pituitary gland to decrease. This mechanism helps to prevent an overload of ACTH. However, additional stressful events can override this inhibitory effect, and cause the pituitary gland to produce more ACTH, which stimulates the production of even more glucocorticoids. Cortisol, one of the glucocorticoid hormones, is commonly used as a measure of stress.

This stress response is very well suited to situations such as running away from a saber-toothed tiger. Most of the stress experienced by our prehistoric ancestors probably came from actual physical threats to their safety. Any perceived danger caused a need to be active and exert energy, such as running away or fighting in self-defense.

As the neocortex of our brain developed, we gained the ability for complex thinking, imagination, and feelings of love, compassion, and awareness. This, in turn, made us susceptible to forms of emotional stress that are unknown in the animal kingdom, such as grief, guilt, and fear about imagined future events. Furthermore, our long period of immaturity and dependency (infancy and childhood) increased our vulnerability to psychological stress.

Our physiological response to stress, however, has not changed. Our bodies respond to purely emotional stress as if we were being chased by a saber-toothed tiger! We are designed to exert considerable energy when we experience strong emotions such as terror or rage. This is not always appropriate, however, and we are left with a physiological stress response that is useless. This can be annoying, for example, when our heart rate goes up before an important interview.

However, this is only a small part of the problem, because *the stress response itself can become damaging in the long run*. In fact, we suffer from a variety of stress-related diseases because of this. Both parts of the stress response (the sympathetic system arousal and the glucocorticoid hormones) can contribute to illnesses.

Repeated stimulation of the sympathetic nervous system can lead to chronic high blood pressure and atherosclerosis (the buildup of fatty deposits in the blood vessels). This, in turn, can cause heart attacks and strokes, two of the major killers, especially among men.[1]

Excess glucocorticoids caused by stress can lead to many negative side-effects, including irritability, apprehension, and the inability to concentrate. But this is only a small part of the problem.

A more serious side-effect of glucocorticoids is the suppression of the immune system. Individuals who are repeatedly or severely stressed have high levels of ACTH and glucocorticoids, and this has been shown to correlate with a lower resistance to infection.[2] For example, adults whose spouses have recently died have a lowered immune response.[3] Stress increases the risk of contagious illnesses such as respiratory infections, as well as immune-related disorders such as multiple sclerosis. Glucocorticoids caused by stress can even accelerate tumor growth.[4]

Excess glucocorticoids can also damage a part of the brain called the hippocampus, which plays an important role in learning and memory. This damage can contribute to learning disabilities and also accelerate the aging process.[5]

Other negative effects of these stress hormones are increased risk of osteoporosis, as well as diabetes in older adults (adult-onset diabetes). Researchers think that both components of the stress response contribute to ulcers, a well-known stress-related illness. Finally, stress can interfere with sexual function by causing impotence in men and inhibiting ovulation in women.[6]

Some of these illnesses also have possible genetic and environmental causes, but the role of stress has been established as a contributing factor.

The physiology of crying

The price we pay for our sensitivity, awareness, and intelligence, therefore, is emotional pain and stress-related illness. What does all of this have to do with tears and tantrums? *It is likely that crying and raging following purely emotional stress evolved as an adaptive mechanism to help reduce the negative side-effects of the physiological stress response.* There is some very interesting physiological and biochemical research on crying that supports this stress-release theory of crying.

In a study of physiological changes during crying, researchers showed female university students a sad film. Those who cried were more physically active than those who did not cry. They also had increased heart rate and skin conductance, indicating general physiological arousal.[7]

Other studies have measured physiological changes *after* crying episodes in adults. The people used in these studies were involved in specific kinds of psychotherapy, during which they cried and raged, sometimes for an hour or more. Measures taken before and after these therapy sessions revealed lower blood pressure, pulse rate, and body temperature, and more synchronized brain-wave patterns after the therapy sessions. These are generally considered measures of relaxation. A control group of people was asked to exercise vigorously for an equivalent period of time, and the same physiological measures were taken after the exercise sessions. However, this control group did not show the same degree of relaxation as did the group of people who cried and raged.[8]

Crying, therefore, is a state of physiological arousal followed by deep relaxation. It is a very effective way to reduce tension and to lower one's blood pressure and heart rate. Perhaps the energy used in crying helps to dissipate some of the energy that is meant to be used to defend ourselves physically against danger, when running or fighting are not appropriate responses. Heavy crying and raging make use of both the sympathetic arousal response and the glucocorticoid response.

It is interesting that the word "emotion" comes from a Latin word meaning "to move." The English language further expresses this when we say, for example, "I was very moved by the film." This implies that our uninhibited, primitive response to strong feelings is to become physically active. Crying and raging in children are indeed very active processes, involving the entire body. Children kick their legs and flail their arms, using a large amount of energy. We adults would probably cry in a similar manner if such a strong display of emotions were socially sanctioned.

In addition to the physiological studies of crying, there are some interesting biochemical studies of human tears. William Frey, a biochemist at the St. Paul-Ramsey Medical Center in Minnesota, has researched the chemical content of human tears.[9] He paid volunteers to watch a sad film and to collect their tears (if they cried) in a test tube. (Imagine being *paid* to cry!) He called these tears "emotionally-induced tears." Later, from the same people, he collected "irritant-induced tears," triggered by inhaling fumes from a cut onion. He then did biochemical analyses on both kinds of tears, and discovered that tears shed for emotional reasons are chemically different from tears shed because of an irritant, such as cut onion. This means that something unique happens when we cry.

Further analyses revealed the presence of certain substances in the emotionally-induced tears that were not present in the irritant-induced tears. One of the substances found in tears was the hormone ACTH (which stimulates the production of glucocorticoids). The implication is that shedding tears helps to reduce excessive amounts of ACTH in the body following a stressful event. This, in turn, probably helps to prevent too much buildup of glucocorticoid hormones. Crying is therefore comparable to other processes such as urinating, defecating, exhaling, menstruating, and sweating, all of which remove waste products from the body.

In addition to ACTH, William Frey also detected the presence of catecholamines in the tear glands and in tears. Examples of catecholamines are epinephrine and norepinephrine. (These are the chemical mediators of the sympathetic nervous system that stimulate the heart to beat faster, increase blood pressure, and increase blood flow to the muscles.) The excretion of these substances in tears would help to reduce the effects of the sympathetic nervous system arousal during stress. He also found a substance called leucine-enkephalin. This is one of several kinds of endorphins (natural opium-like substances) that play a role during stress.[10]

Both of these substances (catecholamines and endorphins) function as neurotransmitters in the brain, which means that they help the nerve cells communicate with each other. These and other neurotransmitters regulate our moods and determine whether we feel happy or depressed. Some psychiatrists think that childhood experiences of stress and trauma can cause disorders in the neurotransmitter systems.[11] It is likely that crying could play a crucial role in restoring a beneficial balance of these chemical substances, thereby reducing symptoms of depression or anxiety without the need for drugs.

Newborn infants typically do not shed tears when they cry until they are several weeks old. However, they do sweat considerably, and they also exert energy. More research is needed to determine all of the physiological effects of crying in people of different ages.

There are several studies that have found a relationship between crying and physical health. The results of a survey showed that healthy people cry more and have a more positive attitude about crying than do people who suffer from ulcers or colitis.[12] In a study of breast cancer patients, researchers discovered that the women who freely expressed anger, fear, depression, and guilt lived longer than those who denied or repressed their painful emotions.[13] There are also documented cases of a relief of asthmatic symptoms and a disappearance of hives when the patient began to cry.[14] Crying is not a cure-all, and should never replace appropriate medical interventions. But releasing painful emotions in a supportive setting can be a helpful addition to a treatment program. Enlightened doctors in the future may recommend the following advice for optimum health: "Eat lots of fruits and vegetables, get plenty of exercise, and have a good cry at least once a week!"

These different areas of research all indicate that crying is a beneficial physiological process, which allows human beings to cope with the effects of emotional stress. When a physical response is not necessary or appropriate, crying helps to reduce the various effects of the stress response. It can be considered a natural repair process that restores the body to a state of equilibrium. Crying is therefore not an unnecessary byproduct of stress, but an important part of the stress-relaxation cycle. When we cry as a response to emotional stress, we release energy, reduce tension, lower our blood pressure, and remove stress hormones and neurotransmitters from our body through tears, thereby restoring physiological balance (homeostasis).

4. THE PSYCHOLOGICAL BENEFITS OF CRYING

Children who cry enough enjoy several benefits. They show improved emotional health, a healthier attachment to adults, higher self-esteem, are easier to live with, and have better learning ability. These five benefits are discussed in this section.

Crying improves emotional health.

Freud's early approach to therapy was one in which he recognized the importance of emotional release such as crying.[1] However, he later abandoned this approach (for unknown reasons) in favor of a more verbal, analytical approach to therapy.

When writing about emotional illness such as neuroses, Alice Miller stated, "It is not the trauma itself that is the source of illness but the unconscious, repressed, hopeless despair over not being allowed to give expression to what one has suffered."[2]

Studies of adults have shown that therapy involving high levels of crying leads to significant psychological improvement. Patients who openly expressed their feelings in this manner during therapy sessions tended to improve more rapidly than those who just talked with their therapist.[3]

Psychologists have studied crying in children during the highly stressful experience of a long hospitalization. Children who protested openly by crying and screaming at the beginning of their hospital stay showed better adjustment than the ones who were "good" patients right from the start. The latter appeared to be calm and cooperative, but were more likely to show signs of stress later on, such as regression to infantile modes of behavior, eating or sleeping difficulties, and learning disorders.[4]

Adults sometimes react inappropriately to situations because they confuse the present with the past. For example, a man may overreact emotionally with rage towards a woman who frequently arrives late for appointments, because she reminds him of his alcoholic mother (who was undependable when she was drunk.) This can happen with children as well. A little boy may be terrified of dogs, even puppies, because a big dog once barked loudly at him.

Psychologists call this phenomenon the "generalization of a conditioned emotional response." *Anything that reminds a person of a previous stressful event will trigger a stress response, even though the new situation is totally harmless.* This had obvious survival value during the millions of years of evolution, when our primitive ancestors faced many physical dangers. Individuals who had a quick and automatic response to potential dangers were the people most likely to survive the longest.

The problem arises when immediate survival is not the issue. With psychological stress, this mechanism is not very useful, because it can interfere with our ability to cope in life and relate to other people. People who have experienced severe trauma often suffer from a condition known as "Post-Traumatic Stress Disorder." Anything that reminds the person of the trauma triggers a physiological alarm reaction, as if the original trauma were actually happening again.[5]

Eventually, conditioned responses wear out if similar situations prove repeatedly to be harmless. When this happens, psychologists call this "extinction of the conditioned response." This can take a long time, depending on the severity of the original trauma and strength of the original response.

However, the process of extinction can be greatly accelerated by emotional release, specifically crying and raging. When children have a chance to cry or rage following frightening or frustrating experiences, the stress response will not be triggered by similar situations later on. The physiological process of crying while feeling safe somehow convinces the brain that the threat has been overcome and resolved. *Crying helps to undo the conditioning of the stress response.* It stops our brains from associating similar events with danger. A child who has cried enough about a dog barking (in the safe embrace of his mother's arms) will react to other dogs cautiously, perhaps, but he will no longer be panic-stricken.

Adults can cry in therapy in order to release emotions resulting from childhood trauma. This helps them to see the reality of the present more clearly and to respond appropriately. A man who can cry and express rage in therapy at his alcoholic mother may still feel irritated when women arrive late, but he will probably not have a rage reaction. It is clear that people will have better emotional health and fewer problems relating to other people if traumatic experiences during childhood can be cried about soon after they occur.

Accepting crying contributes to healthy parent/child attachment.

The British psychoanalyst, John Bowlby, was the first person to use the term "attachment" to refer to a child's bond to his mother. He proposed that attachment behaviors, such as smiling at the mother, clinging to her, crying when she leaves, and following her when possible, reflect the instinctive tendency of babies and young children to seek and maintain proximity to their mothers (or primary caretakers).[6]

Healthy attachments are essential for normal development. Researchers have determined some of the factors that help children form healthy attachments to their parents. During the first year, frequent physical contact with the parents is necessary. Another factor is prompt and appropriate responsiveness to the infant's signals. Children need continuity in caretakers, and they suffer from prolonged separations from their parents, especially during the first five years. Abuse and neglect can also seriously impair healthy attachment.[7]

In addition to these factors, parents need to accept the entire range of their children's emotions in order for healthy attachments to form. Attachment researchers consider crying to be a baby's way of communicating its needs for food, love, and protection. However, they also recognize the stress-release function of crying and the need for empathy during those times.[8] Bowlby pointed out that failure to accept a child's painful emotions can have negative consequences. He claimed that children should be allowed to express their grief openly by crying during situations of separation or loss. He deplored the tendency of some caretakers to tell children not to cry, and claimed that this could lead to painful feelings being shut away from consciousness.[9] He also stated that children should be allowed to express hostile and jealous feelings openly, even those directed at the parents. For example, children should be allowed to say to their parents, "I hate you!" If they are punished or shamed for such outbursts they may either rebel or become anxiety-ridden neurotics.[10]

It is important to respond to a crying child, rather than to reject or punish her. When parents fail to respond to a baby's crying during the first year, the baby may show disturbed attachment patterns. She may be aggressive towards her parents, or excessively demanding or clingy. Some children appear to be self-sufficient and they resist closeness or show lack of affection. Researchers have observed children as young as one year of age who seek communication with their mothers only when they are content, never when they are distressed. Bowlby considered this to be a serious breakdown in communication between mother and child. Children with this extreme avoidant pattern tend to have serious behavioral and emotional problems later on.[11]

Simply responding, however, is not enough when a child needs to release stress by crying. Even though parents may not openly reject a crying child, *any attempts to distract a child away from his crying will be felt by him as a form of emotional abandonment.* Children need parents who are able to listen to their expressions of anger, grief, and fear, and who can empathize with them. If children can openly express these feelings from birth on, they will learn that they do not need to repress painful emotions, and they will feel unconditionally loved.

Full acceptance of children's painful emotions can therefore lead to healthier attachment in the children. Babies who are allowed to cry in their parents' arms will grow up feeling understood and accepted. As teenagers, they will feel comfortable talking about their problems with their parents, and crying if they need to, knowing that they can count on their parents to listen.

In my consulting practice, symptoms of insecure attachment (such as excessive clinging, whining, aggressiveness, or resisting closeness) often disappear when parents are able to create emotional safety in the home and accept their children's crying. The older the children, the more difficult it is for them to feel safe enough to reveal their emotions if their crying has been repeatedly distracted, punished, or ignored. However, it is never too late to improve the parent/child relationship.

Accepting crying increases children's self-esteem.

High self-esteem occurs when children feel good about themselves and confident in their abilities. This follows directly from a healthy attachment with parents because, to have high self-esteem, children need to feel unconditional love and acceptance. If children are shown love and approval only when they are smiling and happy, they will learn to deny and repress a part of themselves in order to please adults. Their deepest emotions will eventually feel unacceptable, even to themselves. Without full acceptance of their feelings and emotional expressions, therefore, children cannot grow up with high self-esteem.

Children who cry enough become easier to live with.

Children who are allowed to cry and rage as much as needed become more pleasant to live with. A long cry or a temper tantrum is not, in itself, agreeable. In fact, it can be quite difficult and emotionally taxing to sit with a child through such an outburst. However, after a good cry or temper tantrum, children are typically happy, relaxed, cooperative, undemanding, non-violent, and self-sufficient.

The transformation is sometimes amazing. Instead of a demanding, whiny, bored, moody, clingy, obnoxious, or aggressive child, adults find that they now have an easygoing child who is a delight to be with. An additional advantage is that babies who cry as needed (while being held, as recommended in this book) become much less demanding and also sleep better at night. This allows the parents to obtain the rest they need.

Children who cry as needed are better learners.

All children are born with tremendous intellectual potential. However, this becomes partially blocked in many children because of experiences of hurt, confusion, frustration, or fear that have not been processed and released through the healing mechanisms of crying and raging. This blockage of intelligence occurs partly because painful emotions occupy the children's attention, lessening their ability to concentrate and learn. For example, it's hard to pay attention in school when your parents are about to get a divorce, and you have no idea with which one you will be living.

There is considerable evidence that stress and traumatic experiences during childhood can have a negative effect on the ability to think and learn.[12] A study of four thousand seven-year-old children found a correlation between stress levels and intelligence. The children with the highest levels of stress had the lowest IQ scores.[13]

In another study, researchers measured the intellectual abilities of Romanian orphans, many of whom had been traumatized through abuse or neglect. These children were delayed in their ability to learn, and this correlated with excess glucocorticoid levels in their blood (specifically cortisol). The children with the lowest intellectual abilities had the highest levels of cortisol.[14] As stated earlier, these hormones are produced by the adrenal cortex during stress, and can damage a part of the brain called the hippocampus. This area plays an important role in learning and memory.[15]

It is not known how much brain damage caused by an excess of these stress hormones is reversible. Crying eliminates excess ACTH from the body through tears, which helps to lower glucocorticoid levels. It is quite possible, therefore, that an acceptance of traumatized children's tears and tantrums could improve their ability to learn.

Children who are allowed to cry and rage whenever they are upset or frustrated are able to maintain an amazing ability to think and learn. In fact, educators have discovered that children become more enthusiastic and successful learners when the need for emotional release is recognized and accepted.[16]

There is another reason why crying can help children become better learners. Children have many frustrations, some of which are directly related to learning situations. These can be easily triggered by later, similar situations. When children are not permitted to cry, these frustrations can interfere with later learning.

For example, a girl with accumulated frustrations about solving puzzles as a child may have difficulty trying to learn geometry in high school. Seeing the different shapes may remind her (unconsciously) of those frustrating puzzles, and trigger a rage reaction. This will make it difficult for her to think clearly, because she is reacting to an imagined source of emotional pain.

These situations can be minimized if children are allowed to cry and rage about frustrations whenever they occur throughout childhood, so the stress response is completely resolved at the time. Children will then approach new learning experiences with more objectivity, rather than with an inappropriate emotional response.

5. THE USE OF CRYING IN THERAPY WITH CHILDREN

Many child psychiatrists and therapists regard crying as a beneficial expression of feelings that has therapeutic value. Some therapists welcome spontaneous crying by children and recognize it as an important part of the healing process. When children feel a sense of trust with the therapist, and know that they will not be reprimanded for crying, they sometimes cry during play therapy sessions.

Other therapists actually encourage children to cry, especially in situations involving loss, because they know that crying is an important and necessary part of the grieving and recovery process.[1]

The role of crying is of particular interest in two therapeutic approaches: birth recovery therapy and holding therapy. These are discussed in the following sections.

Birth recovery therapy

Therapists specializing in the healing of birth trauma with infants find crying to be extremely beneficial. Researchers in the field of pre- and perinatal psychology have found that traumatic births have a potential for causing lifelong problems. There is a correlation between perinatal complications and susceptibility of children to emotional and behavioral problems.[2] Birth trauma may also be partly responsible for later schizophrenia, violent crime, suicidal behavior, and various physical ailments.[3] It is very important, therefore, to help infants resolve birth trauma as early as possible to avoid later problems.

William Emerson, a pioneer in psychotherapy with infants, has developed a successful kind of therapy to help them heal from the effects of traumatic births.[4] One technique he uses is called "Birth-Simulating Massage." The therapist uses touch and pressure on the baby's body to reproduce the sensations experienced during the birth process. Specific trauma areas are given special attention. For example, if a baby was born with the umbilical cord wrapped tightly around his neck, the therapist gently strokes the baby's neck. Infants cry in a healing way during this therapy, and resolve the trauma of their birth. Eventually, the birth-simulating massage no longer triggers heavy emotions.

These interventions are done lovingly and awarely, while the baby is with his parents, and only after the therapist has developed a trusting relationship with the baby. In follow-up studies, Emerson found that children treated with this therapy as infants were very well adjusted and empathic, and showed amazing talents and skills.

Another therapist, Peter Levine, has used a similar technique which he calls "renegotiating birth trauma." He recommends providing an infant with resistance against her feet so she has something to push against, and allowing a build-up of frustration. Then one can place a hand gently on the infant's head. Levine thinks it is important and therapeutic for infants to return to the level of nervous system arousal similar to that which they experienced during the actual birth process. The infant will make use of the resistance provided and push with all her might. The crying that accompanies this is considered to be a release of energy and frustration that was blocked during the actual birth process.[5]

Holding therapy

Holding therapy was first used with autistic children in the 1950's. Autistic children do not relate normally to other people, do not develop normal language skills, and appear to be lost in their own private world much of the time. The causes of autism are not known. However, one form seems to result from an emotional overload due to early trauma, such as birth trauma, prematurity, early hospitalization, or prolonged separation from the mother.

This kind of autism responds quite favorably to holding therapy, in which the mother or a therapist is encouraged to hold the child. The child often resists this closeness, and cries and rages. Several therapists have noted profound and rapid improvements in autistic children after allowing and encouraging them to cry and rage during holding therapy sessions.[6]

Most proponents of holding therapy consider the crucial therapeutic component to be the holding itself. Some feel that only the mother should do the holding. The theory behind this approach is that the child has experienced a rupture in the mother/child bond, and that the holding should be done by the mother to restore closeness. Children resist this closeness at first, and typically go through a phase of intense crying and struggling. They then gradually accept being held, and eventually snuggle lovingly in their mothers' arms. Others feel that a therapist can be just as effective as the mother, and that the trust developed with the therapist can be transferred to the parent/child relationship.

It is possible, however, that it is not the holding itself that allows the child to heal, but rather the physiological acts of crying and raging, which are triggered by being held closely and lovingly. Perhaps the holding allows the child to feel safe enough to relive and release the accumulation of painful feelings resulting from previous traumatic experiences, or simply from an accumulation of stress. Holding gives the child a physical limit to struggle against. This may be an important requirement for healing, especially if the child is dealing with prenatal or birth trauma, or past experiences of powerlessness (such as hospitalization). It also provides a safe "container" for the child's emotions, so the child does not harm himself or others.

Whatever the actual reason for the success of this approach, it has produced dramatic results in many cases of autistic children. There is no single technique that will cure all cases of autism, because this disorder probably has a variety of different causes. However, holding therapy is a promising approach for some children.

Holding therapy has proven to be particularly successful with children suffering from attachment disorders.[7] These are emotional and behavioral problems caused by severe neglect (either emotional or physical), or by repeated changes in primary caregivers, such as occurs when children are frequently moved from one foster home to another. Some psychotherapists include in their diagnosis of attachment disorder children who have been abused by their parents, or who have suffered some other trauma that has interfered with healthy attachment between parent and child

Children with serious attachment disorders either resist forming attachments or show excessive, superficial familiarity with strangers.

They are described as being without a conscience, because they seem to feel no empathy or remorse, and they can be quite destructive or violent: setting fires, killing animals, or seriously harming other children or themselves. These children often lie and steal, and sometimes have delays in language and conceptual skills. Nevertheless, they can seem to be quite "normal" at first contact, and can be deceptively charming.[8]

Children with attachment disorders do not respond well to traditional forms of therapy, because they are unable to trust. Without mutual trust between therapist and child, no progress can be made. Holding therapy allows children with attachment disorders to learn that closeness without pain is possible. Just as with autistic children, holding seems to reach through these children's resistance to feeling loved. Furthermore, it lets them release their painful feelings by crying and raging without being punished, ridiculed, or rejected, thereby healing themselves of the effects of past traumatic experiences. Gradually, they learn to trust.

There is some evidence that hyperactive children can benefit from holding therapy as well: firm but loving holding at times when their frantic behavior is out of control.[9] The official diagnosis of "Attention Deficit/Hyperactivity Disorder" (ADHD) is given to children who are easily distractible, or hyperactive/impulsive. It is estimated that three to five percent of children in the United States suffer from this "disorder."[10]

Distractibility, impulsiveness, and hyperactivity in children can be caused by an overload of stress. Researchers have found that there are higher levels of parental stress in families with children diagnosed with ADHD.[11] Of course, one could conclude that having such a child is a cause of stress. But when the parental stress includes such factors as marital discord, divorce, hospitalization, and substance abuse (as some studies show), one should consider the possibility that the children's behavior is the result rather than the cause of the family problems.

There is also evidence that abused children are often hyperactive, impulsive, and aggressive, and that this is a result rather than a cause of the abuse. In fact, there are many similarities between the symptoms of ADHD and those of Post-Traumatic Stress Disorder resulting from abuse.[12]

Furthermore, many children diagnosed with ADHD also have emotional problems such as depression and anxiety, and some are prone to violence. The causal relationship between these problems and ADHD is not known, but it seems quite plausible that both kinds of problems have a common origin, either in a stressful home situation, or in a history of stress or trauma. (The trauma could be very early trauma, perhaps even prenatal.)

Hyperactive children are prone to temper tantrums, which can be considered a healthy attempt to release stress. Unfortunately, these temper tantrums are often considered to be part of the problem, instead of being recognized as an important healing mechanism. In a pamphlet about ADHD published by the National Institute of Mental Health, tantrums are listed with other disagreeable behaviors: "It's especially hard being the parent of a child who is full of uncontrolled activity, leaves messes, throws tantrums, and doesn't listen or follow instructions."[13] Although nobody would claim that tantrums are agreeable, this sentence implies that tantrums are a part of the problem, revealing a misunderstanding of the potential therapeutic benefits of raging.

I am not claiming that every case of hyperactivity or attention deficit (ADHD) is caused by stress or trauma combined with insufficient crying. However, when these factors are suspected, therapy should include attempts to reduce the stress. In addition, the children can be encouraged to release pent-up emotions through crying and raging. Holding therapy may not be necessary if a hyperactive child is already attempting to release stress through spontaneous crying or temper tantrums.

Martha Welch, a psychiatrist who uses holding therapy, has written a book for parents (*Holding Time*) in which this approach is described for use with normal children.[14] She describes the typical stages in a holding session (confrontation, rejection, and resolution). During the rejection stage, the child typically cries, rages, and struggles to get away. Welch recommends continuing to hold the child. When the resolution stage is reached, there is a complete change from the intense struggle: the child stops crying, relaxes, and becomes loving and tender, often wanting to linger in the mother's arms and continue being held.

Conclusion about therapies with children

The therapies involving crying and raging described in this section are not widely accepted. Many therapists and doctors prefer to avoid anything that triggers intense feelings. Drugs are often prescribed for children suffering from emotional or behavioral problems, even though no neurological cause has been established. Although some children have been helped by drug therapy, the tendency to drug children can prevent the family from looking for possible environmental or psychological causes of the child's behavior.[15]

Even when there is an imbalance in brain chemistry, it is important to realize that this could be the result of trauma.[16] Crying has many physiological benefits, including changes in levels of hormones and neurotransmitters. When children have behavioral or emotional problems, it is logical to give them opportunities to reestablish chemical balance through the natural processes of crying and raging, before resorting to drugs.

The common element in the two therapeutic approaches described in this section is that children are exposed to forms of stimulation that trigger intense emotions. They are touched in ways that trigger a memory of their birth trauma (birth recovery therapies), or they are held closely (holding therapy). In both cases, the stimulus no longer causes resistance, anxiety, or anger after repeated exposure during which crying has occurred.

These approaches are similar to certain exposure techniques used by behavioral therapists for curing phobias. When patients are forced to confront the very situation that terrifies them, they learn that no harm results, and their phobias disappear. In the more intensive exposure therapies, there is often a strong emotional reaction with crying.

Birth recovery therapy and holding therapy are powerful techniques that have the potential for abuse and misuse. Great care must be taken to avoid retraumatizing children during these forms of therapy. Opponents of holding therapy claim that it is abusive and that it can further traumatize a child. Holding should never be done in a spirit of punishment or revenge, or with the desire to harm or dominate a child. If done with awareness and sensitivity, however, holding can produce dramatic positive results.

Dealing with the source of children's problems often means confronting strong emotions. The healing processes of crying and raging are noisy, messy, unpredictable, and time-consuming. They require commitment and attention from caring adults. People are often afraid of strong and painful emotions, and don't know how to deal with them other than to repress them. The next section describes the ways in which crying is repressed.

6. ADULT MEMORIES OF CRYING AS CHILDREN: HOW CRYING IS REPRESSED

Because of the misunderstanding about the importance of crying and raging, adults often discourage and repress these healing mechanisms in children. Your own well-meaning but misinformed parents may have tried to stop you from crying. In my workshops I ask participants to recall what their parents did when they cried. The range of responses is amazing. The most common ones are summarized in the chart below. As you read the rest of this section, try to remember what *your* parents did when you cried as a child.

HOW CRYING IS REPRESSED IN CHILDREN

- Telling child to stop crying
- Punishing (or threatening)
- Withdrawing love or attention, isolating child
- Distracting with talk, music, movement, games
- Putting something in child's mouth (food, pacifier)
- Teasing, shaming
- Denying or minimizing child's pain
- Praising child for not crying
- Getting child to talk or laugh

Many adults remember being punished in some way for crying. Their parents hit, spanked, or threatened them with statements such as, "If you don't stop crying, I'll *give* you something to cry about!"

Another form of punishment is the withdrawal of love and attention. Many people remember being sent to their room for crying. I asked a woman at one of my workshops in Santa Barbara, California, to share with the group how this had made her feel. She started to cry, saying that she had felt lonely and rejected at times when she really needed her mother to hold her. Some parents ignore crying or raging children, because they are afraid of "reinforcing" the behavior by paying attention to it. Another woman shared an extreme example of this at a lecture I gave for teachers at the National Association for the Education of Young Children Convention in Los Angeles. She said that when she cried as a child her mother refused to talk to her for up to a week! It had taken her many years of therapy to overcome the pain caused by such emotional abandonment.

Some people remember that their parents tried to distract them from their feelings by showing them something or suggesting activities, such as a game. Parents sometimes try to get children to laugh instead of cry. Although laughter is beneficial, it cannot substitute for the need to cry. *Crying children should be allowed to continue crying as long as needed.* It is disrespectful to try to change crying into laughter, because it conveys the message that crying is inappropriate, and it trivializes the child's feelings.

Food can be another form of distraction. Feeding children who are upset is a common way of repressing crying: "Have something to eat, it will make you feel better." Parents frequently do this with infants, because it is easy to misinterpret infants' crying. (See Part II, Section 5.)

Some people remember being teased as children for crying. This was usually done by older siblings or other children, but sometimes by parents as well ("Don't be such a cry-baby!").

Many adults remember that their parents often minimized or belittled their pain. Common expressions are: "It's not so bad," "Don't worry," "There's nothing to be afraid of," "There's no reason to be upset," "You're making a big deal out of nothing," "It's not worth crying about," "There's no point in crying over spilt milk." A woman in a workshop in Paris told me that her father used to tell her: "Save your tears for later. You'll need them!" These responses not only stop children from crying (and healing), but they cause children to feel misunderstood and alone with their pain, which is very real for them. Therefore, children can feel emotionally abandoned when spoken to this way.

Adults often tell children to "be a big boy (or girl)," and praise them when they do not cry. A father once said to his son: "I'm proud of you, son. You didn't even cry when you broke your arm." Adults are often eager for children to talk rather than cry. Children are commonly told, "Crying won't get you anywhere," "I can't understand you when you are crying," "Stop crying and tell me what happened," "I won't give you anything until you ask nicely for it," "Use your words," etc. After children learn to talk we sometimes expect them to explain everything with language. Children find it very difficult to put their feelings into words, and it is not at all helpful to ask them to do this when they are crying. If allowed to do so, children cry when they need to, but only as long as needed, and they will talk when they are ready to do so.

Language and emotions are processed in different areas of the brain, with few direct nerve connections between them. Although spontaneous, animated talking does provide a certain amount of emotional release for older children and adults, getting a child to label his feelings is not sufficient to provide a healing release. This forces children to switch from an emotional level to a premature conceptual level, and, if done frequently, could lead to over-intellectualizing tendencies in the child. This cuts the child off from his inner self.

Very few adults were allowed to cry as much as needed when they were young. It is therefore not surprising that parents and teachers have difficulty recognizing this need in children, and providing loving attention when they cry. Do not blame yourself if you feel an urge to stop children from crying. You may catch yourself saying the exact phrases that your parents used with you when you cried as a child. For example, one mother reported that her own mother always told her, "Hush, hush, don't cry," and she finds herself using this exact expression with her son. She never even questioned her response until she was presented with this information about crying in my workshop. It takes time to overcome a lifetime of conditioning. You will find it helpful to take the time to talk with another adult about your own childhood, and to recall specific memories of your crying and how you were repressed. (See Part IV, Section 3: "Dealing with your own feelings.")

The repression of crying often begins at birth. However, most adults do not remember what happened as infants when they cried. Babies cry in order to communicate an immediate need, but they also cry to release tensions and stress. Well-meaning parents often repress this kind of crying, usually by offering some kind of distraction.

One clue to what your parents did with you as an infant is your own response to crying babies. Do you feel a strong urge to put something in the baby's mouth, to say, "Hush, don't cry," or to jiggle the baby? Perhaps you feel like putting her down and walking out of the room. Your first impulse will probably be the exact thing that was done to you as a baby when you cried, even if you do not have a conscious memory of it.

7. DIFFERENCES IN CRYING BETWEEN MEN AND WOMEN

Before adolescence boys cry about the same amount as girls. However, around the age of twelve years there is a sharp decline in crying in boys.[1] This is probably due to both biological and cultural factors. Although there are cultures where men cry more openly and frequently than the men in industrialized nations, in most cultures men cry less than women.[2]

The repression of crying in boys is pervasive in Western cultures. There is no doubt that boys are discouraged much more than girls from expressing feelings of sadness or fear.[3] Boys are socialized to think of crying as a feminine weakness. Strength and masculinity are associated with emotional detachment, rather than emotional vulnerability or sensitivity. Generally, men are very good at talking and analyzing their feelings, but are seldom able to cry, and are often unaware of their deeper emotions. When boys tease each other or younger children for crying, it implies that they have internalized the unfortunate message that it is unacceptable to show strong emotions such as sadness or fear.

The biochemist who studied human tears, William Frey, has suggested that the fact men cry less than women could be a contributing factor to the higher incidence of stress-related illnesses in men (such as heart attacks and strokes), and to the fact that women live longer than men on the average.[4] One study found that men are more likely than women to die following a major life upset.[5] Men don't necessarily experience more grief than women, but women cope with grief more effectively by crying more.

All children suffer from the repression of anger, but this has different effects on boys and girls. Studies have shown that male survivors of child abuse are more likely to become violent towards others, whereas female survivors are more likely to develop self-destructive behaviors, such as anorexia, self-mutilation, or suicidal tendencies.[6] The cultural repression of healthy expressions of anger in hurt children is a possible factor contributing to these distorted expressions of anger in adolescents and adults. The suggestions in this book are therefore important for both boys and girls.

8. CONTROL PATTERNS IN ADULTS

Because most people have had their crying repressed, beginning very early in life, they have learned to hold their feelings in by means of behaviors called "control patterns." These are habits or behaviors that people acquire to prevent themselves from feeling emotional pain and crying. Control patterns often take the form of addictions.

COMMON CONTROL PATTERNS IN ADULTS
(Behaviors to repress crying)

- Consumption of chemical substances
- Overeating
- Nail biting and other habits
- Muscle tensions and rigidities
- Excessive activity
- Distractions (ex: television)

One method used by adults (and adolescents) to repress crying is to consume chemical, mind-altering substances such as tobacco, alcohol, caffeine, or psychoactive drugs (either legally or illegally). These chemical substances act in various ways on the nervous and hormonal systems to create an artificial feeling of well-being or to numb painful emotions. Illegal drugs are considered to be a major problem in industrialized countries today, especially among youth.

Overeating can also be a control pattern. Many people go to the refrigerator or reach for sweets when they are angry or depressed. Compulsive overeating is a major cause of obesity. In the United States one out of every five adults is overweight. People who are overweight are at high risk for medical problems such as strokes, heart attacks and diabetes. Weight-reduction programs usually have only temporary success, unless there is some provision for expressing the strong emotions that arise when people try to change their eating habits.

Another way of holding feelings in is by chronic muscle tension, especially of the face, shoulders, chest, and abdomen, which are the ones used during heavy crying. Chronic muscle tension can be a source of headaches, and can also lead to other problems.

Anything we do repeatedly or habitually to repress feelings can be considered a control pattern. Some people hold their feelings in check by becoming busy and active, while others find distraction from their feelings in front of the television screen.

It is clear that control patterns, besides limiting the expression of strong emotions, can, in themselves, be harmful. However, these behaviors are entirely understandable in a society that inhibits the expression of strong emotions in children. There is no need to blame yourself for any control patterns or addictions that you may have. Most people use some form of control pattern. If your parents had always accepted your crying from birth on, and if you did not fear the loss of your parents' love and attention for showing your painful emotions, you would not have needed to resort to the repression mechanisms that you now have. People have acquired these habits and addictions to survive and cope with daily life by keeping a lid on their emotions.

Because of the misunderstanding about crying, when adults attempt to heal themselves by crying others sometimes think of them as being weak, "falling apart," or "having a nervous breakdown." The medical establishment is very quick to prescribe psychoactive drugs to help people feel better, although these drugs often only mask the problem without resolving the underlying causes. In fact, they often inhibit emotional release through crying and raging, thereby reducing the very behaviors that would benefit the person.

Psychoactive drugs prescribed by doctors may be beneficial in certain circumstances. However, they are sometimes prescribed for ongoing psychological problems that would be better addressed in a supportive setting allowing a healing release of the underlying emotions.

There are many kinds of psychotherapy aimed at helping adults overcome the inhibition to cry by interrupting control patterns, thereby allowing people to resolve early traumas. For the therapy to be most effective, the patients are asked not to take any drugs (including coffee, alcohol, and nicotine) before the therapy begins, so their emotions will not be inhibited. The therapist then helps the patient re-experience early traumas, which is often accompanied by crying and sobbing.

There is a growing field of body-oriented psychotherapies. In these approaches, therapists use light touch, specific deeper pressure techniques, or massage to help people overcome muscular rigidities (control patterns) that could be serving to repress strong emotions. Other forms of therapy involve breathing exercises, or movement and postural change to help a person overcome the inhibition against crying.

When the need to cry is understood and recognized, people can then allow themselves to heal through tears. This reduces the dependence on control patterns. However, some control patterns are more difficult to overcome than others, and many have their origins during infancy. These origins are described in Part II.

(A note of caution: if you wish to withdraw from psychoactive drugs, either legal or illegal, it is advisable to do so under close medical supervision. In addition, support groups are beneficial for all drug-withdrawal attempts, including alcohol and nicotine. The emotional support from a group can be a crucial factor in the success of the withdrawal program, because people often experience strong, unfamiliar emotions that need an outlet.)

PART II:
CRYING IN INFANTS
(Birth to one year of age)

1. EXPLANATIONS FOR CRYING DURING INFANCY

Infants often cry for reasons that appear unrelated to any immediate need. Brazelton has found that young infants cry on the average of one-and-a-half to two hours per day, for no apparent reason.[1] The most crying typically occurs when infants are six to eight weeks of age and then gradually declines. This pattern, so characteristic of infants in Western cultures, has also been found in the !Kung infants of Africa, implying that this phenomenon is not specific to industrialized societies. However, the total amount of infant crying in indigenous tribal cultures is generally less.[2]

Traditional explanations for extensive crying in infants focus primarily on possible physiological causes. The most common of these explanations is that babies cry because they have abdominal pain. The term "colic" originally referred to gas pains, but has come to mean prolonged crying in general. A baby who "has colic" or a "colicky baby" is one who cries a lot. Many people believe that colic results from an immature digestive system or an allergic reaction to some substance in the baby's milk.

There are several reasons why the theory of an immature digestive system is inadequate to explain prolonged crying in infants. First of all, this theory does not fit with Dr. Spock's observation that "colicky babies" usually prosper physically. They gain weight normally, sometimes better than average, in spite of hours of crying.[3] Furthermore, no gastrointestinal malfunction has been found in babies who cry extensively, except in vary rare instances.[4]

Although crying generally decreases with age, many older babies continue to have crying episodes, even though their digestive systems would presumably be fully mature by then. In an extensive survey of crying babies, only 25% had stopped by three months of age, and 25% were still crying at nine months of age.[5]

Abdominal X-rays of "colicky" babies have revealed no gas to be present during the crying episodes, but rather afterwards, as a result of swallowing air while crying.[6] The fact that gas was present in babies after they had stopped crying shows that the presence of abdominal gas is not necessarily painful for babies. So even if a baby swallows some air while feeding, this is not likely to be a cause for crying.

Some people think that allergies and food sensitivities are a possible cause for colic. When infants are bottle-fed, an immediate suspect is an allergy to cow's milk protein. Some babies are allergic to cow's milk, and this possibility should be considered in all cases of extensive crying. However, when 32 normal, four-week-old infants with colic were switched from cow's milk to soy milk, there was no reduction in the duration or frequency of crying, or in intestinal gas production.[7]

Some mothers report that their breast-fed babies cry less when certain foods are eliminated from the mothers' diets. The most commonly cited foods are cow's milk, caffeine, alcohol, eggs, nuts, citrus, legumes, onions, strawberries, grapes, and wheat. However, unless the foods are first eliminated and then reintroduced in the mother's diet to see if the crying increases again, one can never be certain that the mother's consumption of the food actually caused the crying in the first place.

In one study testing the effects of nursing mothers' consumption of cow's milk, researchers found that about 30 percent of babies diagnosed with severe "colic" cried less after all dairy products were eliminated from their mothers' diet. However, a follow-up was done in which half of the mothers of these improved babies were asked to swallow capsules containing cow's milk protein, and the other half were given capsules containing potato starch (the mothers did not know which they were receiving). Several of the previously colicky babies did not begin crying again, even though their mothers had been consuming daily doses of cow's milk protein in capsules. This implies that the cow's milk was not the culprit. The percentage of babies affected by cow's milk was therefore less than 30 percent of the original colicky babies.[8]

Parents with crying babies sometimes resort to what psychologists call "superstitious behavior." If the parents do something different, and the baby cries less the next day, they immediately attribute the reduced crying to their behavior. This attitude is understandable. However, in reality, after eight to twelve weeks of age, most babies begin to cry less, no matter what the parents do.

Because the traditional physiological explanations for crying in infants are inadequate, it is necessary to consider possible emotional causes of crying. I have found it useful to distinguish two reasons for crying in babies.[9] A primary function of crying is to communicate needs and discomforts that require a caretaking intervention, such as feeding, holding, stimulation, or a change in position. When an infant expresses a need by crying, it is the caretaker's responsibility to figure out the infant's need and to satisfy it as accurately and as promptly as possible.

A secondary function of crying in babies is that of stress-release mechanism. Crying allows babies to release the tension resulting from physical or emotional stress. As an example, a baby will cry if an older sibling grabs a toy out of his hand, and this crying may continue even after the toy has been given back to the baby. This shows that the baby is not crying only because of a desire to have the toy, but because of emotional pain caused by his sibling's behavior. The baby certainly feels some frustration and indignation, but perhaps also confusion and anxiety. These emotions are accompanied by tension and arousal, and they need to be released before the baby can return to his calm state and continue investigating the toy. Crying in this example is not the hurt. *It is the process of becoming unhurt.*

The amount of cortisol present in the saliva of infants has been used as a measure of stress. (As mentioned in Part I, cortisol is one of the glucocorticoid hormones secreted by the adrenal cortex during stress, following stimulation by ACTH from the pituitary gland.) Cortisol levels are usually high in infants at birth and during the immediate postpartum period.[10] There is a gradual decrease in cortisol levels until six months of age, after which there is very little change.[11] The high stress level of infants under six months of age helps to explain why crying spells are generally more common during that time.

In order to discover what is stressful for infants, researchers have measured cortisol levels during various situations, ranging from prenatal cocaine exposure to postnatal swim lessons. They have found that *crying itself does not activate the stress response in infants.*

Instead, both crying and the stress response are caused by stressful events.[12]

The goal is therefore not to stop infants from crying, but to minimize the sources of stress in their lives. The following section gives an overview of the various kinds of stress that create a need for crying during infancy.

2. SOURCES OF STRESS FOR INFANTS

You may wonder what is so stressful about infancy that causes a need for crying. It is tempting to think of infancy as a stress-free stage of life with no cares or worries. While this is true in one sense (babies don't have to go to work or pay taxes), it is in reality incorrect. Babyhood is an extremely vulnerable and stressful period of life. Some sources of stress and trauma are obvious, while others are not. There are six major categories of trauma or stress during infancy: pre- and perinatal trauma, unfilled needs, overstimulation, developmental frustrations, physical pain, and frightening experiences. These are discussed in more detail in the following sections.

Pre- and Perinatal Trauma

Specialists in the field of prenatal psychology have shown that babies are sensitive, intelligent, receptive, and extremely vulnerable even before birth.[1] Studies have found that there is more crying in babies whose mothers felt extremely stressed during pregnancy because of emotional, financial, or medical problems, or family emergencies.[2]

Birth itself can be a painful, confusing, and frightening experience for infants, and contribute to later emotional and behavioral problems (as described in Part I). The major kinds of birth trauma are being drugged, removal by forceps, Cesarean delivery, and prolonged labor or oxygen deprivation. After birth, it can be frightening and confusing for the newborn to experience sudden coldness, brightness, rough handling, harsh sounds, or separation from the mother.[3] Medical interventions, such as electronic fetal monitoring, heel sticks, eye drops, and circumcision, are also painful and frightening for infants. I am not advocating abandoning necessary medical interventions. However, it is important to be aware of the emotional impact on the baby of these procedures, and to recognize them as potential causes for later crying.

William Emerson, an expert on prenatal and birth trauma (mentioned in Part I, Section 5), found that 55% of a sample of 200 children showed signs of moderate to severe birth trauma.[4] Babies whose mothers experienced a difficult delivery cry more than babies whose mothers had a less stressful one. One study showed that crying in babies was greater if there had been obstetrical interventions and if the mother had felt powerless during the birth process.[5] Another study showed that babies who had problems at birth were more likely to wake up crying frequently at night during the first 14 months.[6] Crying is greater in newborns following epidural anesthesia of the mother.[7]

Birth-stressed babies are often tense and irritable, probably because of an excess of stress hormones. This explains the sleep difficulties so often seen in babies who had difficult births. The arousal of the sympathetic nervous system during stress inhibits the digestive system. This may lead to feelings of discomfort after feeding in babies who are highly stressed from a difficult birth or other trauma. This brings us back to the colic theory! The cause of indigestion is not an immature digestive system, however, but the baby's own stress response.

By crying, these babies can reduce the effects of the stress response and restore their body's chemical balance. The release of energy during crying is necessary to successfully complete the stress/relaxation cycle. If your baby had a very traumatic birth she may need to cry for an hour or more every day for several months to completely release the stress caused by the birth.

> My son had birth trauma resulting from my unusually long labor (48 hours). As an infant, he always cried when I put clothing on him that had to be pulled over his head. Perhaps this reminded him of the pressure on his head during his long birth. He had many crying spells during the first year that were unrelated to any immediate needs. I held him lovingly and accepted his crying. I noticed that gently laying my hand on his forehead greatly intensified his crying. I assumed that he was working through his birth trauma at those times, releasing the fear and frustration. Eventually I could put shirts on him and touch his forehead with no protesting on his part.

Unfilled needs

A second source of stress during infancy is unfilled needs, specifically those for being touched and held. The first nine months after birth are considered a critical period for the need for physical contact. Babies develop best when caretakers adequately fill this need.

There is an interesting study on the effects of increased carrying on infants. The researchers asked a group of mothers to carry their infants an extra two hours per day. Another group of mothers (the control group) was asked to provide increased visual stimulation. At six weeks of age, the researchers compared the amount of crying by the babies in both groups. The mothers who had been asked to carry their infants more reported one hour less crying per day at six weeks of age than the control group.[8] So, the more babies are held, the less they need to cry.

Babies benefit from close physical contact not only during the day, but also at night. Mothers in traditional cultures usually sleep with their babies. Unfortunately, this practice has been discouraged in technologically developed countries, where babies' need for physical closeness at bedtime and during the night is often disregarded.

In prehistoric times, babies probably slept with their mothers for warmth, protection, and nourishment, just like all other land mammals. Although cultural changes have occurred since then, our physiological and emotional needs have remained much the same. Babies born today are genetically programmed to expect a stone-age, hunter-gatherer kind of lifestyle, and to have their natural needs for being held met by their caretakers.[9] This means that they need close physical contact during the day *and at night*.

Many parents are questioning the wisdom of separate sleeping arrangements, and are returning to the more natural tendency to share their bed with their babies. Some parents report decreased crying after they begin taking their babies to bed with them. Many feel a closer bond with their babies. The practice of the "family bed" is becoming more widely accepted and recommended.[10]

Overstimulation

Information overload is another potential source of stress for infants. Infants are vulnerable to overstimulation because the nervous system is not fully mature at birth. Also, infants lack information about the world, and therefore cannot easily understand and assimilate new experiences. Babies have much to learn, and it is all very confusing at first. Researchers found that bright lights and loud noises were overstimulating for premature infants, while gentle rocking and a heartbeat tone were beneficial.[11] This is not surprising, because infants are accustomed to gentle rocking and a heartbeat tone in the womb.

In many traditional cultures, there is a period after childbirth, lasting up to six weeks, during which the new mother is kept with her baby in a warm, quiet, and dark place, while other women tend to her needs. This guarantees that the new mother will receive adequate rest and time to bond with her infant. It also protects the newborn infant from overstimulation, and allows time for recovery from possible birth trauma. There is usually also close physical contact between mother and infant during most of the first year of life, both during the day and at night. This may help to explain why the babies in these cultures cry less than those in industrialized ones.

Newborn infants in industrialized countries are bombarded with overwhelming stimulation, beginning in a noisy hospital nursery. This continues at home with the sounds of other family members, street traffic, television, videos, computers, radios, telephones, doorbells, toilets, showers, dishwashers, and vacuum cleaners. Furthermore, these babies are often expected to endure these sounds while being separated from their mothers' body with its familiar sounds. It is not surprising that babies in Western cultures cry so much!

Brazelton has observed that fussy periods tend to occur after active efforts by infants to maintain alert and responsive states. He proposed that "this period of active fussing...could then be seen both as a period for discharging overstimulation and for reorganization toward homeostasis."[12]

Many parents notice that their babies cry more following experiences involving new sights and sounds. Here is an example:

> When my son was four months old, we took a six-day trip to San Francisco. This was his first trip and his first experience in a big city. He was very alert the entire time, and did not cry much. However, in the evening of the day we returned home, he cried for an hour and a half in my arms. This was the longest stretch of crying he had ever had. He stopped periodically, but started crying again every time he looked at his familiar bed.

Developmental frustrations

Infants sometimes become very frustrated and cry angrily. This angry crying is not as dramatic as in children over one year of age, and is not usually referred to as a "temper tantrum." However, infants often kick their legs and flail their arms during these crying spells, which can be thought of as miniature temper tantrums.

The intent to master a new skill always precedes the ability to learn it. There is a gap in time between a baby's desire to do something new and his ability to do it. During this gap, frustrations can be expected as a normal part of the learning process. That is why they are called "developmental frustrations." For example, a three-month-old infant may become frustrated when trying to grasp an object because she has not yet learned how to make her hand go where she wants it to go. These frustrations build up and are then released in periodic crying sessions.

Periods of fussiness often precede the acquisition of a new skill, such as the ability to grasp an object or the ability to crawl.[13] So if your baby cries more than usual, she may be releasing frustrations resulting from an intense effort to master a new skill. Be on the lookout for a new ability to emerge!

Physical pain

Physical pain is an obvious source of stress and crying for babies. Researchers have found a rise in cortisol levels in infants following inoculations and surgery.[14] Pain should be considered whenever a baby cries a lot. This is especially likely if the crying lasts longer than usual, or has a different or more urgent sound to it. There may be an underlying medical condition that needs immediate treatment. However, a basic premise of this book is that not all crying is caused by an immediate need or discomfort.

Crying is often attributed to "colic," resulting in a frantic search for remedies. As stated in Section 1, gas pains have not been proven to be the major cause of crying in babies. However, unreleased stress may lead to sluggish digestion and mild discomfort after feeding, because of the effect of the stress response (specifically the sympathetic nervous system) on the digestive system. If a change in position or a gentle massage helps a baby feel better, it obviously makes sense to do this. The underlying problem is not likely to be solved, however, until the baby can release the stress by crying.

Some people attribute crying in babies to teething pain. Teething may make babies a little irritable and clingy, but it is not likely to be severe enough to cause prolonged crying spells. However, in all cases of suspected pain, I strongly recommend trying to alleviate the baby's discomfort before assuming that the baby simply needs to cry.

Other sources of pain and discomfort for babies include the inevitable bumps and bruises as they begin to crawl. In all cases of illness or pain, medical care and treatment should be supplemented with full permission for babies to cry and rage.

Crying resulting from injuries may last longer than the physical pain itself, because there is emotional pain as well (usually fear and confusion). The following example of my daughter illustrates physical pain as the cause of crying that occurred later in the day.

> At nine months of age, Sarah enjoyed going to playgroups with me and interacting with other babies. One morning at a playgroup, I was sitting on the floor with her, and she was nursing contentedly. With no warning, another baby crawled over to us, grabbed Sarah's

hair and pulled as hard as she could! Sarah began to cry, but there were many distractions, and I felt that she did not cry as much as she needed. Riding home in the car, she fell asleep. That evening she cried hard in my arms for about an hour. I noticed that when I gently stroked her hair, she screamed even louder and pushed my hand away from her head. She had never before protested when I touched her head. After crying, she fell asleep peacefully and slept soundly. The next day she did not complain when I touched her hair. She seemed to have resolved the incident.

Frightening experiences

Babies are easily frightened, and this is a possible cause for crying. If you move a newborn too suddenly, and if his arms are not secure, he will become startled and display the "moro reflex." In this reflex, both arms curve suddenly inwards as if to hold on. The infant sometimes begins to cry as well. It is often the reflex itself that startles the infant.

Once infants form attachments, by six or eight months of age, separations from primary caretakers can be frightening. Researchers have found that nine-month-old infants who were separated from their mothers for half an hour had increased saliva cortisol levels, indicating that they were stressed by the separation. However, when the infants were with a substitute caregiver who was warm, responsive, and interactive, their cortisol levels did not increase.[15] Separation anxiety is considered a sign of normal, healthy development. However, it can be a new source of stress in babies' lives, and cause crying in situations that previously did not elicit any protest. (See Part III, Section 5, for more about separation anxiety.)

Babies are extremely sensitive to the mood of people around them. When parents and other caretakers are impatient, resentful, angry, anxious, or depressed, babies will become frightened and confused. A mother's illness or a father's headache can cause a baby to feel anxious, because the parent will behave differently and be less attentive than usual. No parent is perfect. We all have days when we feel stressed and lose patience with children. There is no need to feel guilty about this. However, it is important to remember that this is a possible source of stress for babies, and will increase their need to cry.

I remember a dramatic incident that occurred during a workshop I lead in Santa Cruz, California. This example illustrates how sensitive babies are to the mood of other people:

There were about 20 adult participants and a six-month-old infant. During the workshop, one of the women felt quite ill and went to rest in another room. A few people went with her to take care of her. After a while, one of them came into the workshop room, announced that this was an emergency, and she was going to call an ambulance. At that point a sense of terror pervaded the group, and the baby immediately began to cry. I proposed that we all gather around the mother, who was holding the baby calmly and accepting her crying. After the paramedics arrived and took the sick woman to the hospital, I suggested that everybody find a partner and take turns listening to each other's feelings. Several adults cried during this exercise. Then we took a break, during which we learned that the woman had been dehydrated and was now recovering in the hospital. By this time, the baby had stopped crying. The baby had probably sensed the terror in the room and been frightened by it. Her uninhibited crying expressed the fear that was in all of us. It was a powerful reminder that babies are aware and sensitive little people with intense feelings.

I sometimes wonder what the paramedics thought when they entered the home where we were and saw a large group of adults gathered around a crying baby!

3. WHAT TO DO WHEN BABIES CRY

If you are concerned by your baby's crying, or if you suspect illness or pain, be sure to seek out competent medical advice, because crying can be an indication of a serious condition. The advice in this book is not meant to be a substitute for medical advice or treatment. However, if your doctor tells you that your baby is healthy and that the crying is just normal fussiness or "colic," read on.

The traditional advice for parents was to ignore crying babies, once all immediate needs were filled. Many people believed that there was no harm in letting babies "cry it out," and parents were warned not to "spoil" their babies by responding to every cry. A modified version of this is to leave crying babies in their cribs, but to go to them every five minutes and pat them on the back. This advice is harmful. Babies whose cries are ignored, even for five minutes, feel abandoned, terrified, confused, and powerless. Furthermore, they will fail to develop a sense of basic trust, which is vital for optional emotional growth. ***Babies should never be left to cry alone.***

The other extreme, recommended in more recent parenting manuals, is to pick up babies every time they cry and try a variety of calming methods. The goal is to stop the baby from crying. These methods usually consist of putting something in the baby's mouth (breast, bottle, or pacifier), or providing some kind of rhythmic movement or soothing sound stimulation. These are discussed more fully in Section 5.

My advice is entirely different from either of these two extremes. I recommend always picking up and holding a crying baby. However, once all immediate physical needs such as hunger and coldness are ruled out, the goal is not to stop the crying, but to pay attention to the baby and accept the crying. Then, if the baby needs to release stress by crying, he will feel safe and loved. There is no point in trying to distract the baby from his crying, because this will only postpone it. Once the distraction is gone, the baby will still need to cry. This approach of assisting the crying also establishes a good listening relationship between parent and child right from the start. Many parents don't really listen to their babies or give them the emotional safety and permission to feel or to cry. All human beings need to release emotions, and babies are no exception. It is good for babies to cry, but not alone.

Some parents and caretakers wonder what to say or do while holding a crying baby. The next time your baby cries, and you can't find an immediate need or discomfort, try the following suggestions.

RESPONDING TO A CRYING BABY
(after all immediate needs have been filled)

1. Take your baby in your arms, sit in a comfortable chair, and look at her face. If her eyes are open, look into her eyes. Feel her energy and life force. Hold her calmly, without bouncing or jiggling.

2. Take some deep breaths and try to relax. Be aware of the love you have for your baby.

3. Talk to your baby. Tell her: "I love you. I'm listening. You're safe with me. I will stay with you. It's okay to cry." You can also try to figure out the cause of the crying and verbalize your thoughts: "Did you have a hard day? Maybe we did too much today." Tell her that you understand how hard it is to be a baby. Let her know that you want to help her feel better.

4. Be aware of your own emotions. If you need to cry with her, go ahead. Tell her that you are sad.

5. If she arches away from you or does not look at you, say, "Please look at me. I'm here. I want you to feel safe with me." Gently touch your baby's arms or face to reassure her of your physical presence. Don't be surprised if this causes louder crying than before.

6. Continue to stay with your baby and to hold her lovingly until she spontaneously stops crying.

Many babies, especially young infants, cry with their eyes closed, but they stop crying periodically to look up and check to see if someone is still paying attention. Then, reassured that you are still emotionally available, they close their eyes and cry some more. Others cry with their eyes open and watch you the entire time. It is important to make eye contact when your baby looks at you.

Here is an experience I had with a crying baby who refused to look at me at first:

> I was at a party at a friend's house, and her three-month-old baby started to cry. I offered to hold him, and this was fine with her. She knew that he wasn't hungry. I held him and did not try to distract him from crying. He was soon crying very hard in my arms. I looked at him and tried to make eye contact, but he avoided looking at me. His eyes were either closed or else he looked around the room but never directly at me. His crying seemed chaotic and disorganized. I could tell from his behavior that he was not accustomed to receiving focused attention while crying. It was as if he did not expect me to be looking at him. (He had four older siblings, and his mother did not have the time to pay attention to him when he cried, although she did carry him in a baby sling most of the time.) I kept holding him, touching his head, face and arms, and talking softly to him, reassuring him that I was with him and that he was safe with me. After about 20 minutes of this crying, he began to look directly into my eyes for the first time. He then did some very heavy crying for another ten minutes. This crying seemed more intense and focused, and it relaxed him considerably. After that he fell asleep peacefully in my arms, and I put him down in his bed. A few hours later, after he had awakened and nursed, I said hello to him while his mother held him. He looked directly at me, gave me a big smile, and reached his arm towards me. He seemed delighted to see me.

Though you may feel ineffective when holding a crying baby, in reality you are providing her with much-needed emotional support while she is releasing stress in this manner. To summarize, the important things to give a crying baby are close physical contact, eye contact, verbal encouragement and reassurance, and plenty of listening.

Some parents and caretakers feel rejected by a crying baby, thinking that the baby does not want to be held. Nothing could be further from the truth. Your baby is not rejecting you when she is crying. She is simply feeling safe enough to show you her feelings, just as you might burst into tears if a trusted person were to put his arm around you and acknowledge that you have had a hard day. Parents who hold their babies and allow them to express themselves in this manner notice that their babies are relaxed and content after the crying spell, and sleep longer stretches at night.

During the first few months, you can expect infants to cry at least a few minutes every day, and sometimes for an hour or more. Long crying stretches are more likely if the baby has experienced a difficult birth or other major trauma. If the crying has been repressed for many months, and you are just now beginning to use this approach, you can also expect long crying sessions. Your baby may need to "catch up" on crying that has been previously repressed with various distracting "soothing" methods.

Young infants usually fall into a deep and peaceful sleep after crying, and later awaken bright and alert. After a few months of age, babies don't always fall asleep after crying, but become calm, happy, and alert after the episode.

Some newborns don't start having crying episodes until they are a few weeks old. Perhaps they need all their energy just to adapt to life outside the womb. Once their basic physiological mechanisms necessary for survival are regulated (such as breathing, digesting, urinating, and defecating), they have the resources and strength necessary for resolving emotional stress through crying. This can come as an unpleasant surprise for parents who thought they had an "easy" baby!

Crying patterns vary greatly from one baby to the next, but there are some general trends. Some infants, especially at the beginning, don't necessarily do all their crying once a day. Instead, they have several smaller crying episodes, just as they nurse and sleep frequently throughout the day (and night). After a few weeks, they typically begin saving up their crying for one major crying spell a day. This is often in the late afternoon or evening, just when the parents want to eat their dinner and relax. Some parents jokingly call this the "happy hour."

Many parents notice a reduction in crying between three and six months of age. This may be because many babies have acquired repressing mechanisms by then (See Section 5), and also because of a decreased need to cry. Stress levels are lower in babies after six months of age. By one year of age, even babies who are not stopped can sometimes go as long as a week without crying.

There are large individual differences in the amount of crying, depending on the baby's temperament, sensitivity level, and amount of stress. Increased crying is likely during illness, family conflicts, disruption of routines, overstimulation, and preceding the acquisition of new skills. Many babies need to release tensions through crying before falling asleep, either for a nap or for the night.

Although some parents may claim that their babies cry "all day," this is usually not true. These parents are probably seeing continued fussiness that keeps recurring throughout the day, because they persist in trying to repress the crying. Parents who begin to relax and accept their baby's crying find that the baby cries more intensely, but that the crying does eventually end by itself, and the baby then becomes content and relaxed.

Here is an example:

A two-week-old infant girl was fussy all morning. Her mother was convinced that she had some gas trapped in her stomach, and was unable to burp it up. So the mother tried patting her back, rubbing her stomach, nursing her, and jiggling her, but nothing stopped the fussiness. Finally, at my suggestion, the mother just held her in her arms, looked at her, and gently stroked her forehead. The fussiness quickly built up to a full-blown cry which lasted for about an hour. After that the infant fell asleep and woke up later in a wonderful mood. She was calm and relaxed, and her eyes were very alert. She looked directly at her mother and smiled fleetingly. There was no more fussing that day.

Babies in daycare settings sometimes save up their crying for their parents. This can be baffling. The caregiver reassures the parents that their baby has been perfectly happy all day, and the parents can not understand why their baby cries every evening at home. However, it is natural for babies (and young children) to cry more with their primary caretakers, because they usually feel safer with them.

Part IV (Section 4) has more examples of practical applications of this approach. That section contains many letters from parents who share their experiences with crying infants.

4. HOW TO REDUCE STRESS AND THE NEED FOR CRYING DURING INFANCY

When stress is reduced, babies will have less need to cry. Here are some suggestions for reducing stress and the resulting need for crying during infancy.

TIPS FOR REDUCING STRESS DURING INFANCY

- Strive for a stress-free pregnancy.
- Strive for a drug-free, "low-tech" birth.
- Breast-feed baby if possible.
- Avoid drugs or foods with adverse effects on baby (if breast-feeding).
- Provide close physical contact, both day and night.
- Fill baby's needs promptly; prevent frustrations.
- Avoid overstimulation.
- Protect baby from harm and frightening events.
- Take care of your own physical and emotional needs.

First, try to strive for a stress-free pregnancy and birth. Take care of yourself, eat right, avoid drugs that could harm your baby, and find emotional support. Take childbirth education classes and prepare yourself, as best you can, for a drug-free, "low-tech" birth. If the birth does turn out to be difficult, remember that you are not to blame, and that both you and your baby can heal.

After your baby arrives, try to foster the development of strong attachment through close physical contact. Breast-feed your baby if possible; this is by far the feeding method of choice. You can further fill your baby's need for physical closeness by carrying her in a sling or front pack as much as possible during the day and sleeping with her at night. Do not wait for the crying to begin before carrying your baby. *Hold and carry your baby even when she is not crying.*

If you are a breast-feeding mother, try to avoid taking drugs that could affect your baby, and stay away from any foods that could adversely affect the flavor of your milk or cause a digestive disturbance or allergic reaction in your baby. Be sure to cry yourself when you need to. Many mothers find that they cry more easily than usual during the postpartum period. This is partly the effect of the hormone prolactin, which plays an important role in milk production, but also lowers the crying threshold. Prolactin has been found to act directly on the tear glands. The higher the prolactin concentration in the body, the greater the tendency to shed tears.[1] Perhaps this is nature's way of lowering the concentration of stress hormones in mothers' bodies. This, in turn, reduces the presence of these hormones in the breast milk. When mothers cry, it also helps them release tensions and feel calmer when handling their babies. So don't try to repress your own need to cry. Crying is good for you *and* for your baby.

Do the best you can to fill your baby's needs as promptly as possible. Go to your baby immediately when she cries. Try to figure out what she needs. Feed her when she is hungry (but don't overfeed). Try to prevent frustrations.

Another precaution you can take is to avoid overstimulation. Remember that younger babies are easier to overstimulate than older ones, so be especially careful during the first three months. The best kinds of stimulation for newborns are those that resemble experiences in the womb: gentle rocking, being held snugly, the sound of mother's voice. If you need to take your newborn to a stimulating event, such as a party, you can reduce overstimulation by keeping her close to your body with your familiar odors and sounds. It is best to avoid a move to a new home or major travel during the first six months, if possible. Some babies can handle more stimulation than others. Be aware of your baby's tolerance levels.

Try to avoid being the source of your baby's hurts. Do not yell at, hit, shake, or punish your baby. This will only give her more to cry about. If you leave your baby with other caretakers, choose people who are warm and responsive. Do not leave your baby with strangers if she protests.

Strive to keep family arguments and yelling out of your baby's earshot, but if you do have disputes in front of your baby, make sure that she also sees you resolve your conflict. Do your best to protect your baby from the aggression of siblings.

If there is stress in your baby's life, your baby will need to cry. There is no need to feel guilty or blame yourself if this occurs. You can be very helpful and supportive of your baby's healing process. The main thing to remember is: *don't ever let your baby cry alone.*

5. HOW CRYING IS REPRESSED IN BABIES: THE ORIGIN OF CONTROL PATTERNS

There are several methods for "soothing" crying babies, all of which can result in a suppression of this vital healing mechanism. As previously mentioned, many books for parents have a list of distraction techniques that include distraction by feeding or sucking, by movement (with or without holding), and by various sounds.

Besides these seemingly humane methods, there are the more drastic approaches of giving drugs or leaving babies to cry alone. As already mentioned, some books recommend leaving babies in their cribs to "cry it out." This common advice is given for babies who awaken frequently at night.

I do not recommend any of these methods. Babies should be neither distracted nor ignored when they cry.

Because of these various attempts by parents and other caretakers to stop babies from crying, most babies eventually learn to repress their own crying by means of repetitive behaviors or compulsive actions (control patterns). The repression of crying during infancy is so pervasive that most babies have well-established control patterns by the time they are six months old. These behaviors serve the purpose of repressing strong emotions. Common control patterns in babies include thumb sucking or pacifier sucking, frequent demands to nurse for comfort rather than for hunger, and attachment to an object such as a special blanket or teddy bear.

Most of these methods only postpone the crying by temporarily distracting the baby. The rhythmic and repetitive nature of these methods can effectively "soothe" babies because of the hypnotic effect. Have you ever noticed that babies who suck their thumbs or a pacifier often appear to be in a trance-like state, with decreased responsiveness? However, the tranquillizing effect of these control patterns is only temporary, because they do not allow a release of the underlying, accumulated stress. Control patterns can be considered a form of psychological numbing or dissociation, an activity that allows babies to effectively shut off pain, but not resolve it.

Whatever mechanism you use repeatedly to stop your baby from crying will become his control pattern. He will seem to need that same form of consolation every time he is upset, scared, or frustrated, or when he feels an accumulation of stress. These control patterns can become crutches that will appear to be real needs, but are no different in their effect from adult control patterns or addictions. (See Part I, Section 8.)

Control patterns can be thought of as distorted attachments. Healthy attachments are to whole people. Babies naturally become attached to their caretakers, and this promotes healthy development. When these caretakers are not able to listen to strong emotions, the babies do not feel fully seen or heard, and form substitute attachments to inanimate objects (pacifiers, bottles, special blankets, or stuffed animals, etc.) or to body parts (such as their own thumb or their mother's breasts). These substitute attachments inhibit true intimacy and healthy emotional development.

COMMON CONTROL PATTERNS IN INFANTS

- Frequent nursing for "comfort" (rather than hunger)
- Pacifier sucking
- Thumb sucking
- Excessive clinging
- Attachment to special blanket or toy
- Constant demands for entertainment
- Hyperactivity
- Self-rocking, head-banging

Once established, these control patterns can last for years. It is very difficult to change your baby's habit unless you begin to allow and lovingly accept his crying as described in this book. Once you begin to welcome your baby's crying instead of repressing it, the need for these control patterns will disappear, sometimes quite rapidly. The following sections discuss the most common control patterns and their origins.

Nursing control patterns

Nursing is a common control pattern, especially with mothers who recognize the benefits of close physical contact. There is no doubt that nursing has a temporary, physiological calming effect. This serves the purpose of helping babies relax after feeding, in order to digest the milk better. It would not be advantageous for babies to be active or cry immediately after nursing. They could spit up some milk or swallow air, causing digestive problems.

Some mothers think that nursing is an appropriate way to calm a baby, even though he may not be hungry. Babies who are frequently calmed this way sometimes become chronically fussy and demanding, because they never have the chance for a full-blown cry. Eventually, they become addicted to nursing, and seem to want to nurse every time they are upset for any reason, even after a physical hurt such as a bruised head.

Babies need to cry in order to release the pain resulting from both emotional and physical trauma. Anything that stops the crying is a disservice to the baby, even though it appears to be loving and kind. The need to cry does not disappear when a baby is nursed. It is simply postponed. The tears will need to come out eventually.

In addition to repressing the release of painful emotions, nursing when the baby is not hungry can result in other problems. It can lead to frequent spitting up or indigestion, thereby adding to the baby's distress. Digestive disturbances are even more likely to occur if the baby is already feeling stressed and tense.

Overnursing can be the beginning of a chronic habit of eating when upset. This eating disorder is quite common in adults, many of whom eat compulsively when they are feeling angry, frustrated, or depressed. It is a major cause of obesity.

I have observed that women who overeat are more likely to use nursing as a soothing method for their babies. This is understandable, because they themselves were probably fed at times when they needed to cry. Starting in their very first weeks of life, eating became a way of repressing their own strong emotions. They naturally assume that their babies need the same kind of calming mechanism.

I have received many letters from mothers who were relieved to learn that it was not their job to stop all crying in their babies by nursing them. It is not easy to hold a crying baby and accept the crying. However, mothers almost always notice beneficial changes in their babies after they begin nursing less frequently. (See Part IV, Section 4, for excerpts from some of these letters.)

It is normal for babies to continue nursing for several years, even when nursing is not a control pattern. Babies who nurse for purely nutritional reasons, and who do not use nursing to repress their need to cry, eventually wean themselves. The age of spontaneous weaning depends on the child's temperament, personality, relationship with the mother, and other sources of nourishment in the baby's diet.

In many traditional cultures, mothers nurse the infants very frequently, sometimes as often as several times per hour.[1] This serves the function of a pacifier, repressing the crying. In these cultures there is often considerable crying when the mother weans the child, indicating that nursing had become a control pattern. A !Kung woman from the Kalahari desert in Africa (who had been nursed frequently for several years as a baby) was interviewed about her childhood. She remembered crying extensively during her mother's subsequent pregnancy (when she was weaned) and following her brother's birth:

> When mother was pregnant with Kumsa, I was always crying. I wanted to nurse. Once, when we were living in the bush and away from other people, I was especially full of tears. I cried all the time. That was when my father said he was going to beat me to death; I was too full of tears and too full of crying. He had a big branch in his hand when he grabbed me, but he didn't hit me; he was only trying to frighten me...
> (After the birth): I wanted the milk she had in her breasts, and when she nursed him, my eyes watched as the milk spilled out. I'd cry all night, cry and cry until the dawn broke. Some mornings I just stayed around and my tears fell and I cried and refused all food. That was because I saw him nursing.[2]

Anthropologists usually conclude from observations such as these that the weaning experience itself is traumatic for the children in these cultures. Another interpretation, consistent with the basic premise of this book, is that the children cry after being weaned from the breast because the crying is no longer being stopped by frequent nursing. In other words, the children are "catching up" on crying that has been repressed since birth. The above example shows that this crying, unfortunately, is not well tolerated by adults.

Mothers who respond to every discomfort of their children by nursing them may be projecting their own needs onto their children.[3] For example, a mother may feel the need to compensate for her own unmet needs for closeness, or she may feel the need to repress her child's emotions, thereby keeping her own strong emotions under control. True empathic care involves seeing the infant as a unique individual, separate from the mother, and responding appropriately and flexibly (rather than rigidly) to the infant's physical and emotional needs.

Frequent nursing can also be simply a tradition. Every culture has a different approach to child-rearing, passed on from generation to generation. There is no reason to assume that any culture is better than any other. In industrialized countries the "back-to-nature" approach that imitates some traditional cultures can retain what is beneficial and reject what is not. The fact that mothers in some cultures nurse their babies as frequently as every twenty minutes does not imply that we need to do likewise. If we were to imitate everything done by the !Kung people, for example, we would not nurse babies at all for the first few days, because the !Kung believe that colostrum (the first milk) is poisonous! (Scientists have discovered that colostrum contains extremely valuable substances that have immunologic, laxative, and blood-clotting properties.)

How often do babies really need to nurse? This is a difficult question to answer, because it depends on several factors. During the first month, a full feeding of breast milk requires about two-and-a-half hours for infants to digest. A mother's breasts generally begin to feel full again after that length of time. One can therefore expect young infants to be hungry about every two-and-a-half to three hours (from the beginning of one feeding to the beginning of the next), and to nurse about eight to ten times in a 24-hour period. So a four-week-old infant whose last feeding began at 3 o'clock, and who took a full feeding from both breasts, will probably be getting hungry again by 6 o'clock.

However, this is just a guideline. Babies should never be fed by the clock, but on demand. More frequent feedings may be needed during the first few weeks to build up the mother's milk supply. The following circumstances may also require more frequent feedings: growth spurts, insufficient growth, extremely hot weather, illness, or with babies who are "grazers" (who do not take a full feeding each time they nurse). Babies should be fed whenever they are hungry. But parents need to be aware of the fact that not all fussiness indicates hunger or a need to suck. Nursing should not become a method for pacifying a baby who needs to release tensions by crying.

As babies grow older, the breast milk becomes more concentrated and the babies' stomachs can hold more milk. Therefore, the intervals between feedings gradually increase to four hours or more. Babies who are fed cow's milk formula can go longer stretches between feedings, because cow's milk takes longer to digest. Most babies can go longer stretches between feedings at night. By six months of age, some babies may still need one night feeding. But when babies over six months of age regularly awaken more than once at night demanding to nurse, it is usually an indication that nursing has become a control pattern.

Movement control patterns

Besides nursing, another time-honored method of "soothing" infants is by means of rhythmic movement stimulation through bouncing, jiggling, swinging, or rocking. Movement (vestibular stimulation) is important for infants' development, but if it is frequently used in response to crying, it can result in a suppression of healing through crying. Furthermore, babies can become dependent on this kind of stimulation and eventually begin to provide their own movement when feeling sad, anxious, or frustrated. This could be the possible origin of self-stimulating behaviors such as head-banging, self-rocking, and, later on, general hyperactivity.

Hyperactivity is much more common in boys than in girls. An interesting fact is that parents typically bounce and rock their infant sons more than their infant daughters.[4] It is possible that the frequent movement stimulation for infant boys is a factor contributing to the hyperactivity that shows up later on. This is especially likely if the bouncing or rocking was done frequently in an attempt to stop the baby from crying.

Movement stimulation is important for babies, but the timing for this (as for all forms of stimulation) is crucial. It is best to save activities such as bouncing, swinging, and rocking for times when babies are happy, alert, and ready for stimulation. Do not wait until your baby fusses. Babies do not cry because of a need for these artificial forms of movement. Bouncing and rocking will only distract them from their need to cry.

Some people think that babies need to be calmed with movement because they experienced continuous movement while in the womb. However, there were many times during the mother's pregnancy (perhaps as much as 50 percent of the time) when she was sitting still or sleeping. At those times, the baby experienced only the very subtle movements provided by her breathing. Close holding after birth provides infants with this same subtle movement. If babies cry while being held closely, it is time for either feeding or respectful listening, not frantic attempts to distract the baby. Some mothers resort to jiggling and other artificial movements they would never have considered while pregnant.

If you feel a strong urge to jiggle, rock, swing, or bounce your crying baby, this is probably because of misinformation that you have been given. It may also be a result of your own anxiety and frustration with a crying baby. (A word of caution: don't ever shake your baby, as this can lead to brain damage.)

Pacifiers, thumb sucking and "security objects"

When babies are left to cry alone, rather than nursed or rocked, they develop control patterns that do not require the presence of other people. The most common ones are thumb sucking and clutching special objects such as a blanket or teddy bear. Pacifiers will automatically become control patterns if they are given to infants when they need to cry.

Babies with these control patterns appear to be more independent and less demanding. They simply suck their thumb or pacifier, or clutch their favorite object when they cry. They can usually fall asleep alone when they have their control patterns with them. However, these babies are probably not releasing stress any more than the ones who are frequently nursed or rocked. They are therefore not any healthier, from a psychological point of view. Furthermore, they probably receive less physical contact than babies who have control patterns of nursing or being rocked. This is because their parents assume (perhaps incorrectly) that they are content to be alone.

Some psychologists call these favorite objects "security objects" or "transitional objects." They assume that these objects help children feel secure without their primary caretaker, and make the transition towards independence and self-sufficiency. I prefer to think of these behaviors as control patterns that serve the purpose of helping children repress crying in an environment where they do not feel totally safe to do so. These children are usually harboring pent-up emotions resulting from stress.

When children use these various objects as control patterns, it is helpful to strive for more emotional safety in the home environment, rather than assume that the child is content. (See Part IV, Section 2, for information about creating emotional safety.) Parents who feel comfortable doing so, and are ready to accept tears and tantrums, stop giving pacifiers or favorite blankets to their children once they realize that these objects are repressing the child's feelings. These parents usually see an increase in tears and tantrums, but also a dramatic and immediate improvement in their child's alertness and general mood.

With thumb sucking, it is disrespectful to pull a baby's thumb out of his mouth. After all, the baby has usually decided by himself to suck his thumb. Instead, more indirect methods must be used so that the baby no longer feels the need to suck his thumb. I offer some suggestions in the question-and-answer section of this book (Part IV, Section 5). These same methods can be used with children who use objects, such as a special blanket, to hold in their feelings.

The following example shows that babies will spontaneously take their thumb out of their mouth to cry if they feel safe enough:

> During a workshop that I was leading in the south of France, there was a four-month-old infant who was sucking her thumb. The mother agreed to let me do a demonstration with her. I took the baby in my arms, looked at her face, and gently caressed her forehead. I also talked quietly to her, and told her that it was okay to cry. She soon took her thumb out of her mouth and began to cry. After a few minutes of giving her my full attention while she cried, I looked at the group of adults in the room to explain what I was doing and to answer questions. But as soon as I looked away from the baby, she put her thumb back in her mouth and stopped crying! I told the group that I was going to focus on the baby again, and I predicted that, in response to this attention, she would take her thumb out of her mouth again and cry some more. This is exactly what happened, to the amazement of everyone in the room! During this entire demonstration I never touched the baby's hand that was at her mouth. It was entirely her decision to take her thumb out of her mouth.

How crying is repressed in different cultures

Each culture has its preferred methods for repressing crying in babies. There are cultural control patterns that parents pass on to their children from generation to generation. These patterns result from the living conditions, cultural values and traditions, and the struggles necessary for survival.

As already mentioned, many indigenous cultures use breast-feeding as a pacifier, sometimes nursing their infants as frequently as several times an hour. Infants in these cultures are reported to cry less than those in industrialized countries. However, observers of several cultures have noted that the infants do have crying spells in the evening similar to the colic spells that are so common in Western cultures.

Anthropologists have observed the behavior of !Kung mothers when their infants cried. If the infants refused the breast, the mothers tried rocking them, singing directly into their ears, or talking loudly in an effort to distract them. If these attempts failed to quiet the infants, the mothers walked around with them, rocking, singing, and repeatedly trying to nurse them. Aside from hunger, infants were observed to cry because of overstimulation and frustration in pursuit of a goal. Regardless of the cause of crying, mothers responded to it with nursing, movement, and singing.[5]

In Switzerland, Austria, and Germany, pacifiers are used extensively. This is especially prevalent in localities where people live in apartment buildings, value privacy, and are concerned about disturbing the neighbors. In 1992 there was a pacifier craze in these countries, when it was fashionable for teenagers to wear colorful pacifiers around their necks, and to suck on them.[6] This is not surprising in view of the prevalent tradition of pacifier use with babies in these countries.

Among people who value the development of independence, but are less concerned about noise, such as in the United States, parents are advised to leave babies to cry alone and to send older children to their rooms if they have temper tantrums. These children often learn to suppress their crying by thumb sucking or by clutching a favorite blanket or stuffed animal.

In some cultures, having fat babies is a status symbol that proves good parenting. The parents feed the babies in these cultures whenever they cry, and eating becomes a control pattern. As a result, the babies and children are often overweight, even though the parents may be very poor.

It has been a common practice for centuries to drug crying babies. During the second century BC, the Greek physician Galen prescribed opium to calm fussy babies. In the past, in Europe, parents routinely gave alcohol or opium to their infants to get them to stop crying and go to sleep. One way mothers or wet-nurses did this was by smearing their nipples with lotions containing opiate drugs. The babies would absorb some opium while nursing, and then go right to sleep. Popular preparations containing opium could be easily obtained from pharmacists under the names of "Laudanum" and "Paregoric." Many infants became addicted, while others died from overdoses.[7] A popular, opium-based elixir called "Winslow's Soothing Syrup" was available in the United States without a prescription in the late 1880's.[8]

Another practice in Europe was to soak crying infants' teething rags with liquor, or to let babies suck on a small bag of linen filled with ground poppy seeds (a source of opium) and sugar, or dipped into fermented (alcoholic) cider. In Austria, these early pacifiers used by the farm women were called "Most-Zutz" meaning "cider-tit".[9]

Crying infants are frequently drugged nowadays as well. If there is a justifiable medical reason for a drug, it makes sense to use it. However, many babies are given sedatives simply because they cry a lot, even though there is no known physical cause for the crying. In a survey in England, 25% of babies had been given sedatives by the time they were 18 months old.[10] This was simply to *stop the crying*, not because of a medical necessity. These drugs not only interfere with the vital healing mechanism of crying, but they also make babies lethargic and unresponsive, thereby interfering with parent/infant bonding. Furthermore, babies given sedatives for crying may be at high risk for drug abuse as teenagers. When children's very first attempts to release their painful feelings are repressed with powerful, psychoactive drugs, it would not be surprising if they turned to drugs later in life to cope with their feelings.

It is clear that the repression of crying during infancy is widespread. There seems to be very little understanding of this vital healing mechanism, and very little tolerance for it.

6. HELPING BABIES SLEEP THROUGH THE NIGHT (WITHOUT IGNORING THEM)

Even when babies share the same bed with their parents, night awakenings can be a problem. An understanding of control patterns is the key to solving this problem. If you repeatedly put your baby to sleep by means of a control pattern, he will soon depend on that same crutch to sleep. For example, if you usually nurse your baby to sleep (at times when he really needs to release tensions by crying), he will appear to need your breast each time he awakens at night. This may continue well past the age of nursing for nutritional reasons at night.

Nursing or rocking babies to sleep can cause night awakenings because the babies never have a chance to release tensions through a full-blown cry. Some babies fall asleep quite easily while being nursed or rocked. The parents learn to depend on these methods as an effective means of putting their babies to sleep. This is understandable. Why not do whatever "works" to get a baby to sleep? However, many of these babies start waking up frequently at night needing to cry. The parents think that their babies need to be nursed or rocked again, and this pattern is repeated many times each night, sometimes for several years.

Researchers have found that 20 percent of babies begin waking up at night again between seven and thirteen months of age.[1] A typical pattern goes like this: for the first three months, the baby usually wakes up during the night several times to nurse. This is normal. Babies this age need to nurse every three to four hours around the clock. Gradually, the baby sleeps longer stretches at night, and to the great delight of the parents, starts sleeping through the night. The mother has come to depend on nursing as a convenient way of putting the baby to sleep, and it seems to work. Then, some time around six months of age or later, the baby begins waking up at night again, and the mother dutifully nurses the baby back to sleep. What seems to be a temporary setback continues. Instead of the sleep stretches becoming longer at night, they become shorter.

This situation tests the patience of even the most loving parents. Few people can tolerate sleep interruptions night after night without becoming frustrated, resentful, and exhausted. I admire all the devoted mothers and fathers who tend patiently to their fussy babies at night, always nursing, rocking, and comforting them. I feel sorry for these parents, however, because they do not realize that life could be much easier if they did not always try to stop their babies from crying.

Most parents see only two possible approaches: a) continue to nurse or soothe the baby every time he awakens, or b) ignore him in hopes that he will learn to go back to sleep by himself. As stated previously, the advice to ignore crying babies, even for periods as short as five minutes, is harmful. This can lead to feelings of terror and powerlessness in the babies, and loss of trust.

There is a third response of which surprisingly few people are aware. It is entirely possible to help babies sleep through the night without ever ignoring them when they cry. My first question for parents whose babies awaken frequently at night, is, "How does your baby usually fall asleep?" In almost every case, the baby is put to sleep regularly by means of a soothing mechanism (usually nursing or rocking) that functions as a control pattern. The solution for this problem is to refrain from stopping the baby's crying at bedtime: no nursing, rocking, singing, jiggling, or distractions of any kind. This does not mean ignoring the baby. It implies holding the baby lovingly, but without distracting him from his need to cry. Reassure your baby that all is well and that you understand his need to cry. You are providing safety, love, and attention so that your baby can release accumulated tensions and painful emotions.

Be prepared for the crying to last for an hour or more the first few times, especially if your baby has accumulated painful feelings that have been repeatedly repressed. Stay with him. It's not going to be easy. But after crying, he will relax and be able to fall asleep in your arms. If you wait for another ten to twenty minutes, he will be in a deep sleep, and it will be easier to put him down without waking him up. If you use this approach, your baby should soon start sleeping for longer stretches of time at night without awakening. Some parents have reported immediate and dramatic improvement, while others find that it takes several days before their baby sleeps through the night.

Here is my personal experience with this approach:

When my son was ten months old, I noticed one evening that he was yawning and rubbing his eyes, but he became very active. It was way past the time that he usually went to sleep. I took him to a dark, quiet room and held him close to me. He cried and struggled to get away, but in a few minutes he was sound asleep. This evening hyperactivity occurred periodically after that, but usually when there was a lot of stimulation, such as when we had guests, or following an exciting day. I had also noticed that he could be calmed down and put to sleep if I nursed him. However, he usually awakened during the night when I nursed him to sleep. Nevertheless, I had adopted the habit of nursing him to sleep because it was convenient. By the time he was almost two years old, however, his night awakenings were so frequent (three to six times a night) that I was suffering from lack of sleep. I then stopped all bedtime nursing but held him in my arms while he cried. Within two days he was sleeping through the night. With my daughter, born five years later, I tried to avoid using nursing to calm her down and put her to sleep, but I always held her until she fell asleep in my arms. Frequently, she needed to cry before falling asleep. She never developed a pattern of night awakening.

I recommend this holding approach as a bedtime routine for all babies, whether they wake up at night or not. It fills their legitimate need to be physically close while falling asleep, even if they do not need to cry at bedtime.

When nursing has become a control pattern, some mothers report to me that their babies do not cry well with them, yet cannot seem to settle into sleep while being held unless they are nursed. Or the baby eventually falls asleep, but without having completed the crying that the mother feels is necessary. The baby continues to awaken at night. The explanation for this is that babies who have a nursing control pattern sometimes "shut down" when held by their mothers in the standard nursing position, even though they are not being nursed. This position itself is sometimes sufficient to repress the crying.

I have two suggestions for this problem. One is to hold the baby in a different position than the standard nursing position. For example, you can put your baby on your lap with his back against your abdomen, facing away from you, and you can lean over and provide cheek-to-cheek closeness. This position is different enough so that your baby will not be reminded of nursing, and will not repress his emotions as much as when you hold him in the nursing position. Babies who need to cry will then be free to do so, and may even surprise you with the intensity of their crying.

Another possibility is to have another person, such as the baby's father, hold the baby at bedtime and accept any crying that occurs. Some babies cry much better with their fathers than with their mothers, simply because they associate their mothers' bodies with nursing and soothing. This does not mean that the babies are rejecting their fathers, nor does it imply that they need their mothers. On the contrary, it signifies that they are feeling safe with their fathers, and free to release feelings. Fathers can play an extremely important role in helping babies sleep through the night, provided they can continue to hold the crying baby without becoming too stressed themselves!

Babies who do not have control patterns associated with their mothers' bodies (such as nursing or rocking) may appear to be better sleepers. However, this does not imply that these babies are doing the crying they need to do. Babies who are put in their cribs to settle down by themselves and fall asleep alone, eventually learn to soothe themselves, perhaps by thumb sucking, or holding and sucking a corner of a blanket. These will become their control patterns. When these babies awaken at night, as they probably will, they simply suck or grasp their familiar objects and fall asleep again. This is quite similar to babies who nurse several times a night in order to fall back to sleep. The only difference is that the parents are not generally awakened by the baby who sucks her thumb. However, in both cases, the babies' crying is being repressed.

Helping babies sleep through the night by holding them and allowing them to cry at bedtime can be a lifesaver for families whose stability and sanity are being threatened by a baby who awakens frequently at night. Life becomes much easier when the baby sleeps through the night, and everybody else can get a good night's sleep. Luckily, this can be accomplished without resorting to the harmful method of ignoring babies when they cry. (See *The Aware Baby*).[2]

PART III:
CRYING AND RAGING IN CHILDREN
(One to eight years of age)

1. SOURCES OF STRESS FOR CHILDREN

Children over one year of age continue to be vulnerable to emotional hurts of all kinds. Much of the stress between one and eight years of age is an inevitable aspect of living and growing. Although children in this age range are becoming more competent in making their wants and needs known by language, they still have many developmental frustrations resulting from lack of competence and skills.

As children begin to interact more with other children, their play can cause frustrations and hurt feelings, because children under eight years of age cannot easily understand another person's point of view. They are very self-centered, and only gradually learn to understand the concepts of taking turns or sharing.

New fears also appear in this age range, as children become aware of death and their own mortality. Hearing about violence and watching violent or frightening television or video programs can be sources of stress. Witnessing violence in the home can also be terrifying, even when the child is not the direct target. Separations from the primary caretakers can be very painful for young children.

Sometime during the second year children begin to resist others' attempts to control them, and their emerging sense of self needs to be respected. Children need to be treated with patience and respect, and given some degree of control over their own lives. If you must force a child to do something against his will, it is important to explain the reason for it, then accept the child's legitimate, angry protests.

All forms of punishment contribute to children's stress, because, even if the punishment is nonviolent, it causes emotional pain, and often results in feelings of anger or resentment. In my previous books (*The Aware Baby* and *Helping Young Children Flourish*), there are chapters on effective discipline without using either punishments or rewards.[1] I also highly recommend Thomas Gordon's approach called "Parent Effectiveness Training".[2] The absence of punishment does not imply permissiveness. It is possible to raise and educate children without being either authoritarian or overly permissive, and the results are well worth the effort. The parent/child relationship is better, and the children are more relaxed. As adolescents they will feel no need to revolt.

Children also experience stress when their lives are too hurried or structured. The "hurried child" syndrome is a product of modern times.[3] Adults often rush children from one activity to another, such as school, daycare, sports, clubs, and dance or music lessons. Entertainment for children involves action-packed television or video programs, and electronic games that require quick responses. In former times, life was slower, and there were fewer demands made on young children's time and attention. They had plenty of free time to play and invent their own games out of simple, natural objects. Modern children live life in the "fast lane." No wonder they are stressed!

Many children experience an unstable home situation, because of their parents' divorce, often followed by remarriage. The impact of parental divorce on children is well known. They must cope with feelings of anger, resentment, grief, and guilt at a time when nobody else in the family has much attention for them. Many children then need to adapt to step-parents and often to step-siblings as well. A move to a new home and a change in school can also be very stressful.

Many children also carry around "emotional baggage" (an accumulation of emotional pain) if traumas have not been completely resolved at a younger age. For example, a six-year-old boy whose mother was hospitalized when he was eight months old may have chronic anxiety about losing his mother. This may cause him to cling and cry every time his mother prepares to leave. So even though a child's present life may be fairly free of stress, it is important to remember the possibility of unresolved stress resulting from previous experiences. Parents who adopt abused or neglected children need to be aware of the effects of the past on the children's feelings and behavior.

To illustrate various sources of stress, let's consider an example of a four-year-old girl who is spending the morning at a nursery school. First, another child might knock down her block tower. Then, perhaps she must wait until snack time before she can eat, even though she is hungry. Then this poor child falls off a swing and scrapes her knee. Perhaps she spills paint on her new shoes while painting. Finally, her mother arrives late to pick her up (perhaps triggering in the girl the memory of a traumatic separation during infancy). By the time the mother arrives, this little girl will be in a state of high stress.

2. WHAT TO DO WHEN CHILDREN CRY

The basic premise of this book is that crying helps people of all ages to release stress. As discussed in Part II, it is not always clear when crying is a stress-release mechanism in infants, because they also use crying to communicate their immediate needs. As children begin to express their wants with words, the communication function of crying is gradually replaced by language. The stress-release function of crying, however, is not replaced by language, and this remains an important function of crying throughout life. Once language is fully developed, any crying that occurs is then clearly serving the function of stress-release rather than communication.

Obviously, when a child is upset by an immediate event, such as being stuck under a chair, it makes little sense to stand there and to say, "Go ahead and cry!" *The first step in any situation is to do whatever possible to remove the source of hurt.*

When stressful situations are repetitive, it is also important to remove the source of stress if possible. For example, if a girl continuously teases her little brother, simply allowing the boy to cry on a daily basis will not solve the problem. This is because the cause of his painful feelings is repeated day after day, and is an ongoing source of stress. The entire situation needs to be addressed, and the older sister needs help to stop her hurtful behavior. If a teacher suspects that a child is being sexually or physically abused, the teacher is required to report the family to a child abuse agency. Acting as a facilitator for the child's emotions is not sufficient.

Assuming that you have done as much as possible to remove the source of stress, the next step in any crying situation is to *listen to the child and accept the crying*. In Part II, I recommend that babies should always be picked up and held when they cry. It is not always necessary to pick up and hold children past infancy when they are crying, but they always benefit from aware attention. They often spontaneously seek physical contact when they are crying. They need somebody to stay close, to listen, and to accept their feelings.

Children need our loving presence and attention when they cry because *they need to know that they are loved, no matter how they are feeling*. They need to express their painful feelings without being rejected or distracted, and to know that somebody understands and cares.

Adults sometimes wonder how to listen to a crying child and what to say. I recommend what Thomas Gordon calls "Active Listening": acknowledge children's emotions by stating simply (without analyzing or judging) what you think they are feeling.[1] Few people had good role models for this, which makes it difficult. Furthermore, we so desperately want our children to be happy, that we forget the importance of letting them experience the entire range of emotions.

Here is an example of a very minor hurtful event in the life of my son when he was three years old:

> We had been to the beach and he had found a beautiful shell that he brought home and left on the floor. The next day, he stepped on it by mistake, broke it, and started to cry. I was very tempted to say: "Don't worry, we'll go back to the beach and find another one." But I resisted the temptation, because I would have been trying to talk him out of his feelings. He had a right to express his sadness. So I held him in my arms, and said, "You're very sad because the beautiful shell is broken," and let him cry in my arms as long as he needed to.

It is not always necessary to give a verbal interpretation for a child's distress, especially when you don't know the underlying cause. In fact, the wrong words may cause a child to feel misunderstood. Rather than risk a misinterpretation, it is sometimes better to say only, "You're very sad. It looks like you need to cry." Sometimes a child simply needs someone to stay near as a silent and loving witness to the child's inner experience, which may be too complex to put into words.

3. THE "BROKEN-COOKIE" PHENOMENON

The need to cry gradually builds up until the urge for release is so strong that the child can no longer hold it back. At that point almost anything will trigger tears. Because of this, there are times when the reason for a child's crying may not be immediately evident. The outburst will appear to be totally unjustified by the current situation.

Here is an example: suppose your child is hungry for a snack and you give him the last cookie from a box. This cookie happens to be broken, and your child starts to complain because it's broken. You explain that it's the last cookie in the box. At that point, your child has a full-blown temper tantrum, crying and screaming about the fact that the cookie is broken.

It is clear that being offered a broken cookie is not a hurtful event. The reason that children cry about such insignificant issues is that they have an accumulation of stress. They are making use of minor pretexts to release their tensions.[1] The broken cookie is probably not the real issue at all. In fact, if you allow your child to cry and rage about these minor issues, he will emerge from the crying spell or tantrum quite happy and relaxed. He will probably show no more concern over the "broken cookie."

It sometimes looks very much as if children are trying to manipulate their parents with their outbursts and tantrums. I have met parents who are convinced that this is what their children are trying to do. These parents feel compelled to *do something,* and they think that they have only two choices: a) "give in" to the child and offer him what he wants, or b) get the child to stop this "unacceptable behavior" of using crying and raging to get what he wants.

A change in perspective gives them a new option. When adults understand that crying itself is a genuine need, this behavior no longer looks like "manipulation." There is no need to "give in" to what the child wants when it is a mere whim and not a real need. However, the adult can accept the outburst as a legitimate release of pent-up feelings. Life becomes much easier when parents of crying and raging children realize that *there is no present problem, and they don't have to do anything except be with their child.*

Some adults, who are concerned about frustrating children, give in to children's whims when they are crying, mistaking these whims for genuine needs. In the broken cookie example, a parent may take his child to the store to buy another box of cookies. The result of this indulgent style of parenting is that the children generally become more and more demanding and difficult to live with. This is not because they have been given too much. It is because *they never have an opportunity to release pent-up feelings by crying and raging.* These are children with stress just like all children, but their parents' inappropriate responses to their attempts to release stress have prevented the children from healing themselves.

When adults "give in" after a child has whined and begged for a long time, he is prevented from having a good cry and releasing stress. The child will soon find another reason to whine and beg, and this will continue until he is allowed an opportunity to have a full-blown cry. This is the main mechanism by which permissiveness can lead to children who are demanding and obnoxious.

On the other hand, it is inappropriate to set arbitrary limits and neglect to fill children's legitimate needs, assuming that the children "just need to cry." This would be oppressive, authoritarian discipline. Adults should always attempt to fill children's needs. It is only when children's demands become unreasonable that one must consider the possibility of a need to release pent-up emotions.

Some people claim that children are "asking for limits." They do ask for limits at times. Children feel more secure when they have clear information about what they are allowed to do and what is expected of them. However, when children repeatedly display "testing behavior," it is very often because they need pretexts to cry and rage. Whenever children persist in behavior that they know is not allowed, or repeatedly ask for things that they know they cannot have, it is useful to ask yourself the following question: "Is this child looking for a firm limit so that he can have a pretext for crying in order to release some stress?" If you think this is the case, then saying "No" to the child, kindly but firmly, or providing a physical limit (such as holding) may be quite appropriate. This will allow the child to release pent-up feelings.

Your children's outbursts may be directed at you. Be prepared for this! A very dramatic example of the "broken-cookie" phenomenon occurred with my daughter when she was six years old. Here is what happened:

> Sarah arrived home from school one day and was looking forward to the circus that afternoon, as I had promised. Meanwhile, however, I had changed my plans, and I told her that we were planning to go to the circus that evening, instead. She was not at all pleased with this change in plans, and had a full-blown temper tantrum. She lay on floor, kicking and crying, while screaming, "I want to go to the circus *now*," and, "You're stupid!" Mostly, she kept repeating "You're stupid!" while crying very hard. I was surprised at these words directed at me, because she had never before called me "stupid." However, I was able to listen to her and let her cry and rage. After about 20 minutes, she calmed down, smiled at me, and asked for something to eat. She was in a delightful mood the rest of the day, and that evening she enjoyed going to the circus and wanted to sit next to me.
>
> The next day, I talked with her teacher after school, who told me that Sarah had had a hard day the day before. I asked her what had happened. "Sarah had a big argument with her best friend," said her teacher, "and her friend yelled at her and called her 'stupid'." Then I understood it all clearly. So this was what she had been crying about! It had nothing at all to do with the circus. She had used that as a pretext to release feelings about the argument with her friend.

It would have been easier for me to listen to my daughter if she had said, "Mom, I had an argument with my friend today, and she said, 'You're stupid,' to me. This hurt my feelings, so is it okay if I cry about that and repeat the words she used?" Unfortunately, children don't explain these things! They expect us to understand.

Sometimes outbursts occur at school or daycare centers. Perhaps the spilled juice is a pretext for a child to release an entire morning of accumulated frustrations or feelings resulting from a stressful home situation. The most helpful approach is to allow the crying to occur, even though this may require a tremendous amount of patience from teachers. If the crying is disruptive to the other children's activities, the child can be taken to another room (or a different part of the room), *provided* an adult stays with the child to offer loving support. It is important that children never feel they are being punished for crying or raging.

After children have finished crying (remember, they do stop eventually!), adults can try having a follow-up dialog, but adults usually feel the need for this more than the children do. Teachers can then help provide children with a "dignified" transition back to social activity, while ensuring that other children do not tease them for crying. Keep in mind that the pretext children choose to cry about usually has nothing to do with the real, underlying issue.

4. DEALING WITH PHYSICAL HURTS

Parents and caretakers wonder how to deal with crying following physical hurts, such as a scraped knee or a cut finger. They are sometimes baffled by the fact that children cry much less when the adults minimize the incident. When the adults "make a big deal" of the injury, the children sometimes cry longer and harder. Because of this, some adults have developed the habit of giving only minimal attention to hurt children, out of a fear of somehow causing more crying than necessary.

Children are easily frightened by adults who seem anxious. It is therefore important for adults to stay calm, because it is possible to overreact and to frighten children with our own concerns about their well-being. In this case, the children may cry more than they normally would have, because our own fears give them more to cry about.

I recommend a calm but sensitive approach in which the adult simply gives full attention to the injured child. The adult can acknowledge the child's feelings while accepting any crying that occurs. This can be done while administering any needed first-aid. ("I see you scraped your knee. That looks like it hurts.")

Children sometimes do cry longer when adults pay attention (even when the adults are calm), because the children are feeling safe enough to do so. Researchers have found that people recover from pain more rapidly when they focus their attention on the pain, rather than try to suppress it or distract themselves with other thoughts.[1] Children instinctively know the importance of paying attention to pain.

Furthermore, every accident or injury involves emotional pain in addition to the physical pain. Children may feel angry, frightened, or confused when they hurt themselves. They need to understand why a bad thing happened to them, and their anger needs a target: something or someone that they can blame. For example, if a child falls while riding a tricycle, she might be angry with another child for pushing or for saying "hurry up." There might also be feelings of guilt for having ridden the tricycle in a forbidden area. Perhaps she needs to express anger at the tricycle. ("It's a dumb tricycle, it shouldn't have tipped over.") All of these feelings need to be expressed, and they can last much longer than the physical pain from the scrape or bruise.

> When my son was eight years old, he cut his foot badly on a piece of glass while swimming in a small lake. He cried for a short time, but I was not able to give him full attention because I was trying to keep the bees away from us. At home that evening, he could not go to sleep. He said that he kept imagining the piece of glass slicing into his foot. Rather than try to take his mind off the incident, I encouraged him to talk about it. Together, we imagined the glass cutting through his skin. I also reflected back his feelings, "That must have hurt pretty badly. You must have been frightened by that sudden pain." He cried some more during this discussion. Then he began asking many questions: "Why did it happen to me and no-body else?" "Why did I have to step right on that spot?" "Why do people throw glass into the water?" Finally, he decided that it was the fault of the bees, because he had gone into the water to escape from them! After that he was able to go to sleep.

In addition, physical hurts can serve as pretexts (like a broken cookie) for children to release some deeper feelings. A scraped knee can serve the purpose of triggering accumulated stress. In fact, some children who are accident-prone may be using physical hurts as excuses to do some badly needed crying. Perhaps these are the only times their crying is accepted.

It is a mistake to try to make children talk rather than cry after they have been hurt (except if immediate information is needed from the child for medical reasons). After crying, however, children sometimes need to talk and explain what happened, or return to the place of the accident in an effort to further understand. Children typically continue to talk about their injuries, and will show them to anyone who is interested. It is normal and healthy for children to keep bringing their attention back to their injuries, and to touch or stroke the painful parts of their body.

5. CRYING DURING SEPARATIONS

Separations from primary caretakers are a common cause for crying in young children. These situations are difficult for everybody concerned: the child, the parents, and the other caretakers. It is not always clear what the child really needs, or how to deal with the separation in the most effective way.

Children go through developmental stages that affect how they react to separations from their primary caretakers. During the first six months, most infants do not protest when held by unfamiliar caretakers or left with them. When infants begin to smile, they will smile generously at anyone.

The situation usually changes dramatically between six and twelve months of age, when the first signs of separation anxiety and fear of strangers appear. During the second half of the first year, babies typically reserve their smiles only for familiar caretakers, and often protest when approached and held by strangers. It is no longer a simple matter to leave babies over six months of age with someone else. After this age, they need time to become acquainted with new people to feel comfortable with them.

When one-year-old babies have formed a healthy attachment to their mothers, they typically explore actively in her presence, but use her as a safe base and return to her from time to time. They usually protest strongly when they are separated from her, especially if they are in a strange place, and greet her warmly on her return. These behaviors typical of secure attachment are seen in babies whose mothers have been sensitive and responsive.[1] A similar pattern of healthy attachment can also occur between babies and their fathers (or other primary caretakers).

Separation anxiety is so strong in one-year-olds partly because babies this age do not yet have a concept of the future. They cannot understand that their parents will ever return, even if this is explained to them. All they know is that their parents are gone.

After two years of age, separation anxiety gradually declines as toddlers acquire more language skills and the ability to visualize their parents' return. However, many two- and three-year-olds still have strong separation anxiety, and this is quite normal. Even children as old as eight or nine years may still need time to feel comfortable with new people. There is a natural tendency for children to prefer familiar people, especially during times of illness or stress.

It is important to respect children's legitimate attachment needs. I do not recommend leaving a child with unfamiliar people if the child protests. It is better to take the time necessary for the child to become fully acquainted and comfortable with the new caretaker. This may require more than one visit over a period of several weeks for sensitive and strongly attached children.

Children of all ages deserve to know exactly what to expect. It is therefore important to explain everything to them, no matter how young they are, because they understand language long before they can talk. Tell them where they will be, who will be taking care of them, when you will leave, and who will pick them up. It is then important to do as planned, because changes can be very upsetting to young children.

Children often cry during separations, even when they are left with familiar caretakers. There are several possible reasons for this. A primary reason to consider is that the caretaker may not have good attention for the child. Children who are accustomed to responsive parenting will naturally prefer their usual caretaker to one who is less sensitive to their emotional needs. Some parents notice that their children adapt much more quickly to certain caretakers than to others. Children can be trusted to indicate who is a good caretaker for them and who is not.

Another reason for crying during separations is that the child simply needs to cry because of an accumulation of stress unrelated to separation. Perhaps the child does not cry much with his parents because they often distract him from his tears. When he is separated from them, his built-in distractions are gone, and he is then free to cry. Such a child will appear to have unusually strong separation anxiety, which is actually only a need to cry. The child is not crying about the separation at all, but is simply releasing accumulated stress that he is unable to release in his parents' presence. If this is the case, he will benefit from being left with a familiar caretaker and allowed to cry, provided the person gives him loving support and attention while he is crying. Some children become so dependent on their mothers' presence that they cry when left with their fathers or other well-known relatives. This could be because the mother herself acts as a control pattern for her child. (See Part II, Section 5, for more about this.)

Another possibility is that the separation situation itself reminds the child of a previous, traumatic separation. This can lead to considerable crying during separations, as the child attempts to heal the previous, unhealed trauma. Separations during infancy can have long-lasting effects. Even though infants under six months of age do not usually protest when left with strangers, lengthy separations from primary caretakers should be avoided because they can interfere with the development of secure attachments. A separation from the mother at birth, even for a short period, can be the original trauma that later separations could trigger.

Here is an experience from my own childhood:

When I was three years old, my parents enrolled me in a nursery school. Much to their dismay, I cried every day when my mother left me there. This continued for a full *four months*. I remember feeling unhappy while a teacher held me, but it seemed to me that the teacher always tried to interest me in various activities. As an adult, I figured out a possible cause for this unusually strong separation anxiety. When I was seven months old, my parents had left me for an entire month with my grandparents, who were strangers to me. This is a crucial age at which a strong attachment has formed between a baby and her primary caretakers. A long separation at that age can be very traumatic. My grandparents were not supportive of crying, and neither was my mother when I was reunited with her. I was not separated again from my mother until I attended the nursery school described above at the age of three. The separation must have reminded me of the earlier, traumatic month as an infant, when I did not know whether my mother would ever return. Every day my mother left me at the school, I attempted to heal myself from the previous, traumatic separation that I had experienced as an infant. However, I managed to cry for only a few minutes a day. After four months at the school, I had completed the crying I needed to do, and I no longer needed to cry when my mother left me. If my teachers had paid full attention to me and had let me cry as much as needed the first few days (instead of trying to distract me), I might have cried for one or more hours at a stretch. In this way, I probably could have healed the earlier trauma in less than a week. (When I was four years old, we spent a year in another country, and I adjusted immediately to the new school with no crying at all!)

Teachers usually have considerable experience dealing with separations. They may have a more objective perspective, simply because they are not as emotionally involved with the child as the parents. Teachers can be helpful by explaining to parents about the stages of attachment, and reassuring the parents that their child is showing normal behavior. However, when teachers offer suggestions for dealing with separations, they need to be careful not to minimize or trivialize children's and parents' feelings. Parents should be encouraged to trust their own judgment and to separate from their child at a pace that feels right. The decision about when to leave is ultimately up to them, and they deserve support for their decision.

It is important for parents to express clearly their feelings and needs. Do they want the teacher to hold their crying and clinging child so they can get to work on time? Or perhaps they would like the caretaker to involve their child in an activity while they stand nearby and watch. Maybe they would like reassurance that it is okay to spend the first few days at school with their child.

When children cry during separations, regardless of the underlying reason, this crying needs to be accepted. They should be allowed to express fully their grief, anger, and anxiety. Difficult as it may be for the adults, it is far better for a child to cry freely than to have her feelings denied, belittled, ignored, or distracted.

To avoid a crying scene, some parents wait until their child is happily involved in some activity, and then sneak out the door when she is not looking. I do not recommend this approach, because it will only lead to mistrust, insecurity, and more clinging in the future. It is better for children to know when their parents leave, and to face the issue of separation, even though it may be distressing for them. Remember that the separation itself may be only a trigger for the crying.

The following example illustrates a mother's inappropriate attempts to stop her son from crying during a difficult separation, and the caretaker's supportive listening to the boy's crying. This is the caretaker's account of what happened:

> There was a little boy (three years old) whose mother was very concerned and protective. He knew me, but I had never taken care of him before, and he had never been to my house. When his mother brought him to my house, he started crying and didn't want her to leave. She said, "Now stop that. You be a good boy, don't cry, that's enough." But he kept crying, and she sat down with him and promised to bring him cookies and a candy bar. Then she said, "You know you're not supposed to cry like that. You're a big boy, you're not a baby." Of course that made him cry worse. Finally she decided to leave and said, "I'll be back. Stop crying." I said, "Don't worry about it. I don't mind his crying." As soon as she left, I held him and he cried and cried. At first he resisted being held, and I said, "You're sad because your mommy went away. You're a little scared. You don't know me very well. Your mommy is going to come back in a little while. It's okay if you cry. You can cry as much as you want. You'll feel better. It's all right. I know you want your mommy and you're scared." He cried for about twenty minutes. He didn't struggle for more than the first minute or so, and then he let me hold him. He seemed relieved to be able to cry. Then he was just fine, very happy, and he played with the toys and began talking to me. I'd never heard him talk before. Every time I had seen him, he had been very quiet and fearful. So it was very rewarding when he just started chattering away, happily telling me things.

Some children have unusually strong and persistent resistance to separation, even when they are left with very familiar people, because they sense their parent's anxiety. If you are the parent of a child with unusually strong separation anxiety, it may be helpful for you to explore your own feelings during separations. Perhaps you have valid concerns about your child's physical safety or emotional well-being in your absence. If you have concerns or questions, it is important to discuss them with the new caretaker. However, if your anxiety persists, it may be wise to look for another setting for your child.

If you are reluctant to leave your child with anyone, a possible reason for this may be that you are reminded of past separations in your own life. If you lived through a traumatic separation from your own parents as a child, or if you have experienced a miscarriage, stillbirth, or death of a child, it is very natural to feel anxious about separating from your child. However, if you suspect that your own resistance to separation is having a negative effect on your child, it may be helpful to work through your feelings with a competent therapist.

If your child shows a sudden refusal to stay with a familiar babysitter or relative, even though she was formerly quite happy to be left with that person, you should look for the possible causes. Perhaps the child is frightened by a new dog in the person's home, or maybe the person has been less attentive to the child. Maybe the child was spanked or yelled at. Do not overlook the possibility of physical or sexual abuse. Children need to be trusted. If they are suddenly and strongly resistant to being left with a specific person, *they should not be left.*

To conclude, there are three important guidelines to keep in mind when dealing with the confusing issue of separations: a) Babies and children have a genuine and legitimate need to be cared for by familiar people who are sensitive to their needs. They should never be left with total strangers if they protest. b) When left with caring people who are familiar to them, children cry for several possible reasons, such as distress resulting from previous painful separations, or an accumulation of stress. c) Regardless of the underlying cause for the crying, children need warm, loving support, and plenty of listening and acceptance of the need to cry.

6. DEALING WITH VIOLENCE

There is a huge concern about violence in the world today. What causes violence? Why do some children hit or bite? And how do sweet little babies turn into gun-carrying gang members, murderers, and terrorists?

There are two basic conditions that produce violent tendencies in human beings. One condition is that *the person has been hurt*. A child who is spanked, hit, beaten, or threatened with violence will have a tendency to become violent himself. Sexual abuse and emotional neglect are also hurts that can lead to violent tendencies. The accumulation of minor hurts (stress) can lead to violent behavior as well. The anxieties, disappointments, and frustrations of childhood can build up and cause a child to hit or bite.

The second basic condition is less well understood. *The person has not been allowed to release the emotions resulting from the hurts.* He has unresolved and unexpressed feelings about what he has experienced. Only then will he have a tendency to be violent towards others. Being the victim of violence and other distressing experiences breeds violence in the child only when the emotions are blocked and repressed. When this situation occurs, violence toward self or others is almost an inevitable outcome. Violence is a distorted expression of the person's rage or terror in an environment where it is not safe to reveal or release strong feelings.

Added to these two basic conditions is the fact that violence is tolerated and glorified in most industrialized countries, and is culturally linked to appropriate male behavior. Children are exposed to violent male sports, and to television programs, films, and electronic games with mostly violent male protagonists. Little boys are given toy soldiers, guns, and other war paraphernalia with which to play. Story books and school text books often glorify war, a predominantly masculine activity, and describe great male conquerors as heroes. Many parents are pleased when their sons fight back in self-defense with playground bullies, and adults worry about boys who refuse to fight. Combined with the fact that boys are expected to be tough and not cry, it is not surprising that men commit more violent crimes than women.

If we were to purposely design a culture with the goal of producing violent people, we would create it exactly like the culture in which most modern boys grow up.[1]

To prevent violence, we must, first, stop perpetrating violence on children. This means no spanking or hitting. We also need to protect children from violent scenes on television or videos. We must change the messages about violence that we give to boys, and expect the same standards of nonviolent behavior from boys that we expect from girls.

Furthermore, both boys and girls *must be allowed to cry and rage.* Otherwise, they harbor unresolved anger, resentments, frustrations, and fears that they may act out as violence toward others or themselves. Crying can be very effective in dissipating aggressive energy.[2] Much of the emotional pain of childhood is an inevitable part of growing and learning. Children get hurt and experience stress even with the most caring parents and teachers. It is therefore vitally important to allow the natural healing mechanisms of crying and raging.

In view of this, how can an adult respond to a child who is acting violently? The child must have experienced some kind of physical or emotional pain, and he must have been unable to release his feelings. Therefore, violent children need to be encouraged to cry and rage. If a child is about to hit another child with a wooden block, you can grab the child's arm and stop him before the act with a loud "No!" This method of firmly stopping the violence can serve as the necessary pretext that will trigger a healthy release of tears and rage from the would-be aggressor.

Here is an example, told to me by my sister, who frequently took care of a five-year-old girl (whom I will call Janice):

> One day when I was with Janice, she was whiny, and Laura (the mother) was busy, with no more patience or attention for her daughter. So I suggested to Janice that I would stay with her if she wanted to go in the back yard with me. She eagerly agreed to go outside. While Laura was doing laundry in the house, I sat with Janice outside and paid attention to her. She was still whiny and upset. She picked up a long stick and started trying to hit me with it. I caught it each time before it reached me, so I wouldn't get hurt, and I said, "I'm not going to let you hit me with the stick." After a

while I held onto my end of the stick instead of letting it go, and she pulled and pulled, trying to yank it away from me. At this point she started saying, "Let go, let go," and finally burst into tears, sobbing and crying with great intensity while we both held onto the stick. This continued for a while until Laura, hearing her daughter cry, came out on the back porch and said in an irritated tone of voice, "Why don't you give her the stick?" She thought that I was provoking Janice to tears. So I let go of the stick. Janice stopped crying, but then *put the end of the stick back into my hand*, started pulling it again, and resumed her crying! This was a clear indication to me that she needed to cry, and that she needed me to hold the stick so she could pull on it.

At other times, firm but loving holding may be the only way to stop a child from acting violently. If an older sibling is pushing or hitting the baby, you may need to hold the older sibling firmly, explaining that you cannot let him hurt the baby. If you keep holding him, he will probably struggle and protest, but if you persist lovingly in maintaining physical control of him, he may eventually channel his anger into tears, and cry it out in the safe embrace of your arms. You can say: "I know that you sometimes hate your little sister and feel like hurting her. I understand how you feel, but I need to keep both of you safe now, so I'm going to hold you for a while. I'll listen to your sad and angry feelings. It's okay for you to cry if you need to."

The key with anger and violence is to help the child feel safe enough to release feelings by crying instead of acting out the feelings through hurtful behavior toward others. Whatever allows the child to feel loved and safe will help her channel her violent urges into healing tears. At the same time, the violence needs to be firmly interrupted to prevent any harm from being done. Firm but loving holding accomplishes both of these: it stops the violent behavior and provides the closeness and love necessary for the child to feel safe. If done with awareness and sensitivity, holding can be extremely effective and beneficial.

Here is an example of the effective use of holding, told to me by the mother of a three-year-old boy:

I'm beginning to know when he needs to cry. For example, this morning I could tell that he needed to cry. He did not wake up very happy. He was kind of grumpy and he hit me. What finally trig-gered some heavy crying was when I wrapped him in a towel and he wanted to get out. That did it. I just held him and he screamed and cried. I didn't hold him so tight that he couldn't move. I let him struggle and wiggle, but I just kept him in it. I said, "I just want you to stay here for a few minutes," and he cried and cried and screamed and kicked and struggled. I let him out of the towel at one point, but then he turned around and threw something at me. So I bundled him right back up again and he continued to cry. After having held him in there for perhaps ten minutes, I let him out and he was a changed child. None of that grumpiness, but all smiles. He was just fine. I asked if I could hug him, and he put his arms out and gave me a hug. Then I knew that he had cried enough.

Some adults resist using holding in this way because they feel it is oppressive to hold a child against her will. But these same adults may not hesitate to send a child to her room against her will (an approach known in the United States as "time-out"). They then often use threats of further punishments to prevent her from coming out. Sending a violent child to her room may produce short-term results. However, this will only make the underlying problem worse, because it causes the child to feel abandoned, misunderstood, and unloved. That is why I recommend loving holding rather than isolation or withdrawal of attention.

Although violent children usually resist closeness at first, they really do want to be held, as the following examples illustrates:

I frequently took care of a two-year-old boy whom I had known since his infancy. At two years of age, he began to hit other chil-dren when he was frustrated. One day, after he had hit another child, I took him in my arms and held him firmly but lovingly. He struggled to get away and began to cry, saying that he missed his blanket (a favorite blanket that he usually carried everywhere with him.) I kept holding him while listening and acknowledging his feelings. He soon stopped struggling and sobbed in my arms for an hour, and then fell asleep. For several days after that incident he was not at all violent with other children. However, a week later, he became frustrated with another child and grabbed a wooden block with the intention of hitting the child on the head. As he raised his arm, I yelled, "No!" He looked at me, dropped the block, came to me, and said, "Hold me!" I held him in my arms and he began to protest and struggle to get away. However, I kept on holding him and he soon began to cry. His resistance gradually diminished and he cried trustingly in my arms for an hour and a half. Afterwards he was relaxed, happy, and non-aggressive.

This example helped me realize that children really do want to be held even though they sometimes struggle to get away. They need the reassurance that there is something stronger and more powerful than their rage. This stronger force is the adult/child bond. Holding an angry child is like providing him with a sturdy container into which he can pour his emotions. However, *holding should never be used as punishment or revenge, or with the goal of making a child submissive or obedient.* If done with compassion and love, holding will not lead to resentment in the child.

I occasionally used this kind of holding with both of my children. If I maintained my hold until the crying ceased by itself, they were always in a delightful mood afterwards. They often wanted to continue cuddling with me, even though they had been struggling to get away only minutes previously. After a crying session during which my six-year-old son had protested vehemently against my holding him closely, he stated, "I like your way of cuddling because it helps me get rid of something."

When teachers and caregivers consider the use of holding with violent children, I recommend obtaining the parents' permission, as for any other approach to discipline. Holding is most effective if done by a person who has a close, loving relationship with the child. It is a very useful and effective alternative to punishment, both at home and in a nursery school or daycare setting. Holding sets a limit on the child's aggressive behavior without harming the child, and allows a genuine healing to take place.

The use of holding for children who hit, kick, scratch, or bite is described in a book written for teachers, published by the National Association for the Education of Young Children. The following excerpt describes holding, and explains why this is a better approach than hitting a child:

Use your hands and arms and body to hold the child in your arms
or in a small room with you. The child will benefit by your control
and by your understanding, will finish with the outbreak, and will
be all right. The child will remember, next time angry feelings
come up, that you are not an enemy and that you have ways to help
establish self-control...Occasionally, you may find it necessary to
hold children's arms if they try to strike you, or grasp their chins if
they try to bite you, or place your ankle over their legs if they try to
kick you. If you do this only to control children's actions, because
you believe that it would be wrong to strike them, they are safe and
you are safe. Both of you will come out of the crisis able to work
together and with respect for each other.[3]

Some adults try to redirect violent behavior. For example, a child
who is hitting his baby sister can be given a doll to hit instead, or
allowed to punch a pillow. A child who bites a friend can be encouraged
to bite a rubber toy or an apple. This redirection of the violence toward
other targets can help temporarily to protect the would-be victims. It
can also let the aggressive child know that his feelings have been
acknowledged and understood. However, this does not usually resolve
the underlying feelings unless the child also cries and rages. Because
violence is so often a distorted expression of terror or grief, the physical
acts of hitting or biting are not likely to bring a genuine relief from the
painful feelings involved. A jealous sibling who has been hitting or
biting will best overcome her anxiety about losing her parents' love
once she can sob deeply within the safe embrace of her parents' arms.

Sometimes children direct violence at their parents. There are
several possible explanations for this. It can be an indication that the
parents have been hurtful toward the child, perhaps punitive,
authoritarian, unfair, impatient, disrespectful, or neglectful of the
child's legitimate needs. Stopping the child's violent behavior is
certainly justified, but examination of the adults' behavior is also
needed, because it could be a source of the child's aggression.

No parent is perfect. Because of this, *all* children feel occasional
rage toward their parents, especially the primary caretaker. In
children's eyes, mothers alternate between being goddesses (when the

mother is feeling relaxed and loving) and monsters (when she loses patience or becomes inattentive). Furthermore, parents must set necessary restrictions for reasons of health and safety, such as removing a sharp knife from a child's hands, or putting the child in a car seat when riding in a car. When children are angry, they need to be stopped from hitting, but should be allowed to protest openly by crying and raging and saying, "I hate you!" *They need to know that these feelings will not cause the parent to reject them.*

Some children who try to hit their parents may simply have an accumulation of stress (unrelated to the parents' behavior), and need a firm limit to release the feelings. Hitting can be the child's way of asking for assistance in releasing strong emotions, as in the preceding examples. Holding the child can be an effective way to set a limit and provide a pretext for the child to cry and rage, thereby allowing a harmless outlet for the child's aggression.

To summarize this section on how to deal with violence, children who act violently are always suffering from painful emotions. There are effective and non-punitive ways to stop violent behavior while helping the children release the underlying feelings. *It is important to know that children need the most love and attention when they act the least deserving of it.*

7. BEDTIME CRYING

It is quite common for children to need to cry before they can relax and go to sleep. Some children find a pretext for crying (the "broken-cookie" phenomenon). For example, a little girl may cry for twenty minutes because one of the bathtub toys is broken or because she hates the taste of the tooth paste (that she never complained about before). Another child may provoke a sibling to the point where both children dissolve in tears. This evening crying allows children to release accumulated tensions before falling asleep. Children who have cried enough fall asleep more quickly and sleep better at night.

Some children become hyperactive in the evening, and benefit from a reduction in stimulation and distractions so they can settle down. It is well known that quiet, dark places are more conducive to sleep than bright, noisy ones. If this does not help, it is possible that the children will benefit from firm but loving holding so they can find relief in tears. This crying will then be followed by deep relaxation.

Another common bedtime problem is that a child cries when left alone, but stops crying as soon as a parent comes into the bedroom. In Part II, I explain that infants have a genuine need for the physical presence of another person when falling asleep and also during the night. Children over one year of age continue to need this closeness, and some bedtime problems can be resolved by meeting this need. When a child cries after the parent leaves, this may be a legitimate protest against being left to fall asleep alone.

I recommend staying with children at bedtime until they reach an age when they no longer request this reassurance. Holding your child in your lap, or lying down next to her until she falls asleep, are very loving and effective ways to help her go to sleep. This provides security and an opportunity for children to talk or cry about the upsets of their day.

As children grow older, it becomes easier to leave them before they fall asleep, provided they have had the occasion to talk and release feelings as much as needed. The age at which children can fall asleep without an adult present varies greatly, and depends on children's temperament and the living situation. Children who share a bedroom with siblings are generally more likely to go to sleep without an adult close by. Children with vivid imaginations have more intense fears, and may need an adult close by at bedtime at an age when their less creative siblings can fall asleep happily alone.

Parents who sleep with their infants wonder at what age they can move their child into his own room. This is something that each family needs to work out on an individual basis, depending on everybody's needs.

Times of illness or stress may cause not only an increased need to cry but also temporary setbacks in children's ability to sleep alone. It is normal for people of all ages to seek proximity to attachment figures when they are feeling stressed.[1] Under extreme stress, even teenagers benefit from closeness at night. At the age of 13, Anne Frank moved into hiding in Amsterdam with her family to escape the persecution of the Jews by the Nazis. She wrote in her diary that she crawled into bed with her father when she felt afraid at night.[2]

8. HELPING CHILDREN HEAL FROM SPECIFIC TRAUMATIC EVENTS

There are times when the cause of stress is a specific, known, traumatic event. Children experience many such events in their daily lives. Some of these are mild. For example, a friendly puppy jumps on a child and frightens him. Other traumas are more severe: a child must be hospitalized, or there is a fire in the neighborhood. In cases like these it is beneficial when parents and other caretakers have the skills for helping the child resolve the traumatic experience.

To avoid later problems, it is best if adults allow children to cry as much as needed immediately following traumatic events. After a hurricane hit the United States South Carolina coast in 1989, parents of 278 young children living in the area were interviewed six to eight weeks later. These parents reported that their children had many symptoms, including more crying spells and temper tantrums than before the hurricane.[1] This increased crying can be considered an attempt by these children to heal themselves.

When children are discouraged from working through the trauma in this manner, or if the trauma was very severe, they may show symptoms of Post-Traumatic Stress Disorder that can last for years. These symptoms include nightmares, night awakenings, specific fears, anxiety, hyper-arousal, regression to previous stages of development, difficulty in concentrating and learning, and recurrent, intrusive thoughts ("flashbacks").[2]

Parents and other caretakers can be very helpful with children suffering from specific traumas (although I recommend professional therapy as well, in cases of severe trauma). Children often spontaneously bring up traumatic events in their play. This is an indication that they are attempting to resolve them. Sometimes, however, children avoid anything that reminds them of the trauma. In this case, adults can gently help them focus their attention on it, while taking care not to overwhelm them. Some people have the misconception that it is kinder to refrain from discussing traumatic events with children, in the hope that they will soon forget them. However, avoiding the memory of painful experiences will not help children resolve them. The healing processes described in this book allow children to complete the stress/relaxation cycle that has been locked in place by insufficient emotional release at the time of the trauma. The three basic principles of emotional healing are described below.

HEALING FROM EMOTIONAL TRAUMA

1. *Children need to feel secure and loved.* They need to have a trusting relationship with somebody and know that the person will not hurt or abandon them. Physical closeness and aware attention help children feel safe.

2. *Children need to recall the trauma and re-experience it to some extent while feeling safe.*

3. *Children will spontaneously talk, laugh, engage in therapeutic play, cry, rage, sweat, or even tremble* when there is a proper balance of attention between feeling emotional safety in the present and experiencing the emotional pain from the past. These are important healing processes that are most effective when they are accepted by an attentive listener.

Infants resolve stress and trauma primarily through crying while being held. As mentioned in Parts I and II, adults can help infants work through birth trauma by providing them with gentle physical reminders of the birth process in a loving and supportive way.

As children grow older, they make use of other stress-release mechanisms as well, specifically talking and playing, accompanied by laughter. Adults can encourage children to tell the story of what happened by talking or through play. Therapeutic play is facilitated by appropriate toys and supportive attention, as described in the following examples.

If a puppy has jumped on a little boy and frightened him, the first thing to do (once you have assured the child's physical safety) is to accept the child's crying without attempts to distract him. If allowed to cry fully at the time, he will resolve the emotional trauma.

However, if the boy is stopped prematurely from crying, he may develop a fear of dogs. You can help him overcome this fear later on by playfully reenacting the scene with a stuffed dog, or encouraging the child to pretend to be a dog while you act frightened. Anything that elicits laughter will be therapeutic in helping the child overcome his residual fear of dogs. Laughter is a release of fear, and can be very helpful when crying has not been completed.

You can help a child resolve the stress resulting from hospitalization by giving her a doctor's kit and letting her play with it. She will probably laugh if you let her be the doctor while you play the role of a frightened patient. Or you can pretend to be an incompetent doctor who makes silly mistakes, to help your child release tensions and fears through laughter. You can also encourage the child to express anger at a puppet doctor, or show tender loving care for a sick doll. Through play, children can master and control terrifying or confusing experiences, thereby gaining new perspectives.

Following traumatic experiences, children sometimes make use of the "broken-cookie" phenomenon, finding pretexts to cry heavily. (See Part III, Section 3.) These may be related to the original, traumatic incident. For example, a boy who is afraid of dogs because of a traumatic incident may use the sound of a dog barking as an opportunity to cry about dogs. In this manner, he will spontaneously complete the crying he needs to do.

A girl who has recently been hospitalized may cry unusually hard about scrapes and bruises for a few weeks after returning home. If you can remember that she is using these minor injuries as pretexts for resolving the larger, traumatic experience of being sick in a hospital, it will be easier to be supportive during these emotional outbursts. The child is not overreacting, she is healing herself.

Sometimes the pretext that the child chooses to cry about is unrelated to the traumatic incident. The following example of my daughter illustrates this:

> One day, we had a major fire in our city that destroyed over 300 homes, but not ours. The next day, we drove around to see the

damage. That evening, my eight-year-old daughter refused to put on her pajamas because she was sure a spider was hiding in them. I turned the pajamas inside out to show her there was no spider, but she cried very hard for an hour, saying she was "too scared" to wear them. Finally, she put them on. Her fear of spiders was not new, but it had never been this strong before. I assumed that she had created the idea of a spider in her pajamas to help herself release her terror about the fire.

When children feel sufficiently safe, they can heal themselves of even the most traumatic experiences.

PART IV:
PRACTICAL APPLICATIONS

1. INTERPRETING CHILDREN'S BEHAVIOR

Babies and children who have been hurt or have an accumulation of stress will spontaneously attempt to heal themselves through the stress-release mechanisms of crying and raging. However, they will do so only if they feel loved and accepted. A feeling of safety is required before the natural stress-release mechanisms can function. Orphans who live in insufficiently staffed institutions or refugee camps typically cry very little. It is common for these children to begin having frequent crying spells after they are adopted into loving families.

As discussed in this book, well-meaning adults often discourage this natural process of crying because they are unaware of the beneficial effects of allowing the process to continue without interruption. The previous sections describe how this repression of crying may begin at birth and continue into later years. Consequently, many children do not cry as much as needed.

There are several behaviors that suggest inadequate crying. Some of the most obvious ones are the control patterns. These are the various habits that children adopt to repress their emotions. Some common control patterns in infants and young children are frequent demands to nurse purely for comfort (rather than for hunger), thumb sucking, pacifier sucking, and attachment to an object such as a special blanket. These behaviors become unnecessary once sufficient emotional release has taken place.

Other possible indications of a need to cry include disagreeable behaviors, such as hitting or biting, excessive clinging and whining, and obnoxious or repeated "testing" behavior (purposely doing something forbidden). Furthermore, children who are hyperactive, easily distractible, or overly impulsive may also be suffering from an accumulation of stress with insufficient emotional release.

Adults often consider these various behaviors to be part of a child's inherited personality: "She's a real clinger," or "He's got that aggressive tendency, just like his dad." Symptoms of hyperactivity, impulsiveness, and distractibility are often considered symptoms of a mental disorder in the United States, and may be diagnosed as "Attention Deficit/Hyperactivity Disorder." (ADHD.) (See Part I.)

When these various behaviors are considered to be possible signs of stress and an indication of a need to cry or rage, new ways of helping these children emerge.

Children who have been allowed to cry freely since birth (with loving attention) are more likely to be emotionally healthy than those whose crying has been repeatedly repressed. Emotionally healthy children do not need control patterns of any kind. They love to cuddle, but they use nursing (or bottles) only for nutritional reasons, not as a means to stop themselves from crying. They do not suck their thumb or a pacifier, and their happiness is not dependent on a special blanket or stuffed animal. These children are generally happy and alert, loving and cooperative. They have a much longer attention span than is generally considered normal for their age, and they are naturally curious and eager to explore and learn. They are resourceful and full of initiative, and they never willfully harm anybody or anything. These children are very comfortable in their bodies, tension-free, and well-coordinated. They generally sleep well, but do not require much sleep.

Emotionally healthy children are not necessarily easy to live with, however, because they are not passive or docile. On the contrary, they know what they need and can be very persistent in getting their needs met. Furthermore, all children are somewhat egocentric until the age of seven or eight years, because they cannot easily understand another person's point of view. Healthy children are highly sensitive, and have intense feelings, both positive and negative. They cry and rage as needed when they have been hurt, scared, or frustrated, or following a stressful day. After crying, they become again happy and alert.

If a child does not fit this description of emotional health, he or she could be reacting to ongoing stress or to an accumulation of past, unresolved stress. I recommend asking the following two questions:

a) How can this child's life be made less stressful?
b) How can you create an environment of emotional safety so that the child can release pent-up emotions?

This second question is the basis for the success of this approach, and I answer it in the following section.

2. CREATING EMOTIONAL SAFETY

When children display behaviors that show a need to release painful feelings, parents and caretakers may wonder how to help them feel safe enough to let the feelings out. The following is a list of guidelines that can help children open up emotionally and cry and rage as needed. I also recommend these same guidelines for children suffering from severe trauma (but not as a substitute for professional therapy).

GUIDELINES FOR CREATING EMOTIONAL SAFETY

- Give children plenty of physical closeness.
- Give children plenty of aware attention.
- Listen respectfully to children when they talk.
- Stay close and pay attention to children when they are crying or raging.
- Use a non-authoritarian approach to discipline.
- Give children correct information about crying.
- Communicate your own feelings and needs honestly.
- Deal responsibly with your own strong emotions.

Give children plenty of physical closeness.

Hold children frequently, let them sit on your lap, and cuddle with them. Be sure to provide this even when they are not feeling upset. With infants, provide as much close physical contact as possible: carry them in a sling during the day, and let them sleep in close physical contact with their primary caretaker at night.

Give children plenty of aware attention.

There is a special kind of undivided attention that is useful in creating emotional safety. With children under the age of two years, it is best to be available with this special attention whenever the child requests it. After a child reaches two years of age, the adult can set aside a certain time period when it is convenient. An example might be every day after the evening meal for 30 to 60 minutes. The guidelines for these "special times" are the following:

a) Pay attention to only one child at a time. Be totally available, at the child's level, with your full attention on the child.
b) Let the child initiate all the activities and decide how to spend the time with you. Do whatever the child wants you to do (within reasonable safety limits). Even infants will initiate activities if allowed to do so.
c) Avoid directing the play with your own ideas, or turning it into a teaching situation.

This kind of special, non-directive attention gives children a sense of security, which allows them to bring up painful feelings in a play context and work through them. One child may initiate a game of hide-and-go-seek to work on separation anxiety. Another may want to play doctor in order to overcome fears of injury, illness, or death.

Children know what they need in order to heal, and they will do so spontaneously, with the help of an adult's aware attention. These non-directive, special times with children help to create the emotional safety needed for deeper feelings to come to the surface.

Listen respectfully to children when they talk.

When children talk, listen and respond politely, just as you would with another adult. Do not interrupt children, and avoid talking about them to someone else when they can hear you.

When children talk about their feelings, acknowledge and accept the feelings, whatever they are. Reflect back the child's feelings, to let him know that you are listening and that you understand ("Active Listening"). Don't ever tell a child that he or she should be feeling differently, and resist the urge to minimize the feelings. Be especially careful not to belittle fears and sadness in boys or anger and indignation in girls. Avoid giving advice or changing the subject.

Stay close and pay attention to children when they are crying or raging.

Whenever children cry, make sure they feel loved and accepted. Acknowledge their painful feelings. *Never withdraw attention, attempt to distract, or otherwise discourage a child from crying or raging, even if the child seems to be "overreacting."*

Use a non-authoritarian approach to discipline (without punishments or rewards).

Nobody can feel emotionally safe in a relationship based on a power imbalance, where behavior is controlled by punishments and rewards. However, this does *not* mean that adults should become too indulgent or permissive. The role of adults is not to discipline children through power and control, but to fill children's basic needs and provide emotional support, protection, information, and guidance. (See my two books, *The Aware Baby* and *Helping Young Children Flourish*. I also recommend Thomas Gordon's book, *Parent Effectiveness Training* and his home video instruction course).[1]

Give children correct information about crying.

Comment compassionately about other children who are crying or raging. Explain that the crying child is feeling very upset (sad, angry, scared, etc.), and that the crying or raging will help him feel better. It is also important to clarify misinformation about crying in children's stories, nursery rhymes, songs, and on television and videos.

Communicate your own feelings and needs honestly

Adults can improve emotional safety by being honest and open about their own feelings, rather than dishonest or self-sacrificing. A useful approach is to begin by learning to use "I-messages" rather than "you-messages."[2] An "I-message" states how you feel without criticizing, judging, or blaming the other person's behavior. A "you-message" criticizes the other person ("You are messy," "You are bad," "You are selfish," etc.).

For example, you can say, "I feel worried when you leave your toys on the living room floor, because I am afraid that I might stumble over them." These statements even can be strong, such as, "I *hate* crumbs in my bed!" Giving children "I-messages" helps them learn to understand another person's point of view, and it makes conflict-resolution much easier because they have information about how their behavior affects others. It also provides a model for being open with feelings. I have learned that when I remember to use "I-messages" with my children, they often respond with strong "I-messages" of their own.

Deal responsibly with your own strong emotions.

Being with a crying or raging child can bring up strong feelings in adults. Children have an amazing ability to sense who is emotionally available for them and who is not. They save their deepest feelings for those people with whom they feel the safest. If you feel angry, impatient, embarrassed, anxious, or powerless when children cry, they will probably not feel totally safe with you. The following section discusses ways of dealing with your own strong feelings that are triggered by a crying child.

3. DEALING WITH YOUR OWN FEELINGS

The recommendations in this book are not easy to put into practice because of the strong feelings triggered in adults when children cry or rage. These feelings are frequently intense and unpleasant, ranging from mild annoyance to violent urges. Some adults feel deep concern, compassion, and even grief when they are with a crying child. Others feel powerless or incompetent.

These strong emotions often have their origin in childhood. Most people were discouraged from crying as children. This means that most adults have a backlog of their own unresolved stress and trauma. When you hear a child cry, it can trigger an unconscious memory of your own childhood pain (grief, anger, fears, jealousies, frustrations, etc.). It can also trigger an unconscious memory of your parents' response to your own attempts to cry as a child. This triggering effect causes people to feel uncomfortable, perhaps even angry, when children cry, and to either ignore their crying children or respond to the crying with the same inappropriate methods used with them. This is understandable, because it is natural to imitate one's role models, whether they were positive or negative. We have a strong tendency to repeat what was done to us.

It is possible to treat children differently from the way you yourself were treated, but it is not easy, because it requires conscious effort and commitment. If you find it difficult to accept crying or raging in children, and would like to change your usual response, here are some suggestions.

Talk about your feelings and your childhood.

When parents have repressed painful childhood experiences, they are more likely to repeat the same harm with their own children. A first step, therefore, is to become aware of what went on during your own childhood.

I recommend finding another person to talk to, who can listen well and empathize with your feelings. Some people find journal writing to be helpful. Begin by recalling specific memories of crying or having a temper tantrum as a child. Describe what you were crying about, what your parents did, and how you felt about it. It is also helpful and therapeutic to state what you really needed in the situation. How would you have liked your parents to respond? In general, did you feel accepted and understood by your parents? Were they able to tolerate certain strong emotions but not others?

It is also important to express the feelings you experience when your child is crying. It is normal to feel occasional anger or resentment toward your child. Such feelings are quite common. If your parents hit or spanked you for crying, you will feel a strong urge to stop your own children from crying in similar ways. Do your best to resist this urge. But don't be ashamed to talk about it, and to share with someone else the fantasies you have of wanting to harm your child. If you can release your angry feelings in a supportive, therapeutic setting away from your child, you will be less likely to act them out with your child.

As you explore your feelings with a supportive listener, you may become aware of trauma from your own childhood that is not directly related to crying. Some parents are afraid of becoming abusive towards their children because they themselves were abused as children, so they prefer to ignore their own children when they cry. Some are afraid of "giving in" to their children because they themselves had very little control over their own lives as children. Perhaps your baby reminds you of a younger sibling who cried a lot and took your mother's attention away from you. It is important to express whatever feelings are triggered by your child's crying. You can take turns with a partner answering the questions on the following page.

Try to regain your own ability to cry.

Therapists have discovered that talking about one's childhood is not always sufficient to bring about positive changes in one's parenting skills. It is necessary to remember and re-experience the repressed emotions, such as anger and grief. Abusive and neglectful mothers were able to respond more lovingly to their own babies only after they themselves began to release pent-up grief and anguish for themselves as neglected or abused children.[1] So don't be afraid to grieve for your own unmet needs as a child.

EXERCISES IN SELF-AWARENESS ABOUT CRYING

These questions are most useful if they are answered aloud with an empathic listener who avoids judging or giving advice.

1. What did your parents do when you cried or had a temper tantrum as a child? Try to recall specific incidents. Were you punished, reprimanded, teased, ignored, soothed, or distracted? If so, how? How did you feel about that? How would you have liked your parents to respond?

2. How do you feel when your child cries or rages and you can't find an immediate reason? Try to recall a specific incident.

3. Does your child remind you of someone else when he or she is crying? Who? (a younger sibling, a needy parent, yourself as a child, etc.). How does this resemblance affect your response to your child's crying?

4. How do you feel when your child cries around other people? Has anyone ever commented on your child's crying or lack of crying? ("What a good baby!" "He a real crybaby!" "She's so sweet tempered.") How did it make you feel?

5. Did you ever see an adult crying when you were a child? What were the circumstances? How did it make you feel?

6. Have you ever had a good cry and felt better afterwards? Recall a specific incident. Have you ever had supportive listening from another person while crying? How did it feel?

Find a partner or a therapist with whom you can cry. Join a support group in which crying is accepted. Or cry alone if this feels beneficial. A woman at one of my workshops said that she puts on a sad video when she needs to cry, and then has a good, releasing cry while watching it.

Parents often wonder whether it is harmful for them to cry or rage in front of their children. In general, I recommend saving your release of strong emotions for times when you are away from your children. Some children become very upset when their parents cry.

However, I also think that crying in front of children can be beneficial in providing a role model for releasing feelings, provided you reassure the children of the following three things: a) you are not "falling apart," and are still able to pay attention to them and take care of them, b) they are not the cause of your painful feelings, c) you do not expect your children to counsel you or take care of you. Children should never be made to feel responsible for adults' feelings, nor should children be used as therapists. Some parents cry with their children. This is fine, provided they follow the above guidelines.

Be especially careful with expressions of anger. Many adults do not know how to express anger appropriately. *Yelling and screaming should never be directed at a child.* If you feel the urge to yell, it is best to do this away from children and to muffle the sound in a pillow.

Get help and support, and fill your own needs.

If you are overwhelmed or exhausted, with little time for yourself, children's crying will be especially difficult to tolerate. Look for ways to fill your own needs. Some mothers think that they must sacrifice their own needs for their family. This will not benefit the family in the long run, and will lead to inevitable feelings of frustration and resentment. You are entirely justified in asking for whatever help you need.

If you find yourself harming your child, you need immediate help. Don't hesitate to call a child-abuse hotline, or join a support group. There is nothing shameful about doing this. It can be helpful to meet other parents who are also trying to cope with the effects of their own violent childhoods and the stresses of parenting.

To conclude, children do not need perfect parents, but they do need parents who are following a path of self-discovery and healing, and who can recognize and repair their mistakes. Having children provides us with a unique and wonderful opportunity to understand ourselves better and to heal the pain from our own childhoods.

4. PARENTS SHARE THEIR EXPERIENCES

I have received hundreds of letters from parents who have read one or both of my previous books (*The Aware Baby* and *Helping Young Children Flourish*). This section contains excerpts from a few of these letters, illustrating some practical applications of this approach. Many of these parents wrote about the emotions (both positive and negative) that they experienced when they began to accept their children's feelings. (All names have been changed to protect the identity of the writers.)

Parents learn to relax when their baby cries.

I first read *The Aware Baby* some years ago (before I had any children) with very mixed feelings. Now I am a mother, and I understand better what your book is all about.

One evening, when our Joanna was three weeks old, my husband was bothered by the tension I was generating trying to keep her from crying: jiggling, moving around, etc. I remembered your theory and, although I was still skeptical, we decided to try it. I forget now how long she cried that very first time while we held her, maybe half an hour. I remember she suddenly went from red and very loud to pale and very relaxed. She slept longer at a stretch that night than any other night until then (five or six hours, I think), and was so happy the next day.

With some support from other people, and rereading *The Aware Baby* a month or two ago, we have been increasingly comfortable about Joanna's crying. There have been times when she hasn't needed to cry much at all, maybe once a week. Other times, it's been more often. She's apt to be very quiet and well-behaved out in public, and "cuts loose" only at home.

If people comment on her, beyond saying how big or beautiful she is, they are apt to say how alert and aware she is for her age (she just turned four months yesterday). Which, of course, reminds me of your theory.

Neither John nor I are particularly bothered by her crying. If anything, I am a little bothered by how un-bothered I am! The most difficult part for me was trying to reconcile this theory with nursing on demand. There was a while when Joanna was nursing *a lot*, gaining weight very fast, and I kept changing my mind, wondering if I was nursing too much. To my relief she has slowed down. I still usually will check whether she wants to nurse before deciding she's ready for a cry, although it's easier to tell the difference now.

A placid baby begins to express anger.

I read your book (*The Aware Baby*) when my son was two months old. He never really cried but he was fussy and a restless sleeper. He also nursed very frequently, especially after stressful events, like out-of-town visits, holidays, etc. Sometimes it seemed like he was nursing day and night for two days. I nursed him more to "comfort" him than to feed him. But he really didn't get comforted at all. He was a mellow, peaceful baby, supposedly. He just nursed all the time. Everyone told me he was so "good."

So it bothered me when I read your book. On some level I wondered if maybe he was a little too placid. I felt you were correct. He needed to do some crying. I needed to let him know it was okay for him to cry. At first it was a little crazy. I'm insecure about it because I don't know anyone who mothers like that. All my friends either "comfort" their babies with the breast or entertain them to get them to stop crying. And many women I know leave their babies in the other room to cry it out. I definitely abhor that idea. So I'd cry with him. I felt that whatever I'd do would be horrible. I was a little frantic for a while.

I've been letting him cry in my arms for about three weeks and he sleeps more soundly and nurses so infrequently, I sometimes worry. But he looks just great. Right away he began using his thumb as a substitute for my nipple to keep from crying, but that's going away too. Also, I'm glad that he's venting his feelings. I grew up feeling I was a "bad" child because I threw temper tantrums and raged. I also learned at an early age that anger is antithetical to love. I'm unlearning that now. I want to hear if my son is angry at me (or sad, or whatever). He's a person too. I'm strong enough to handle that and still love him.

Another thing, hearing my son cry has brought up a lot of pain for me from my childhood. I think it's a good cleaning out. I feel somewhat deprived when I compare my situation with my son. When I give him permission to cry and still love him, I cry because I remember how sad I felt that my mother didn't give me unconditional love. She didn't meet my needs as I am meeting Alan's. She didn't take my feelings into account. It's good to see my child as a little person with all kinds of wonderful emotions, and to find the beauty in sharing his pain as well as his joy.

Parents thought they had an ideal baby.

We read your book about a month ago, when our baby, Joshua, was about eight weeks old. Your ideas excited us because of their congruence with personal development methods with which we are familiar. Being already convinced of Freud's discovery that in order for healing to occur one must have recall with affect, and having seen this demonstrated many times in rebirthing experiences (using the Stanislav Grof method), we decided to test your ideas.

We thought that Joshua was an "ideal" baby: placid, seemingly contented and happy to entertain himself on a lambskin rug for a part of each day. Although he had low birth weight after a Cesarian section at 39 weeks (because I suddenly developed severe toxemia and the placenta was not functioning properly), he gained weight from day one, and was at the 50th percentile for weight by about eight weeks. At that time, we estimate that he had cried for a total of only about ten hours.

We had attributed his good nature to the relaxed approach we had to parenting. However, Joshua was seeking food every hour or two hours in the late afternoon and early evening. So, after reading your book, instead of offering him the breast, I held him and gave him my full, loving attention, but no food. After about ten seconds, he burst into a fully fledged cry and continued to cry heartily for about 20 minutes with his eyes fixed trustingly on me whenever they were open. After this session, he dropped off to sleep and awoke very alert and contented, and played by himself on a rug for an hour or so with an aura of calmness about him. Each day since, he has cried for five to 90 minutes. Afterwards, he is always calm, alert and very smiley.

One of the interesting features of his crying is its similarity to our observation of people experiencing sadness or anger in rebirthing sessions. It seems that a few minutes after the crying has begun he drops from a more superficial level (which may perhaps be about a specific issue) to a deep level which appears to touch an existential sorrow. The calmness that follows these deep cries feels similar to the wonderful transpersonal, spiritual experiences we have enjoyed in rebirthing and meditation.

We believe that there are many links between your work and parts of the transpersonal movement. It seems to us that the ideas in *The Aware Baby* offer children the possibility of reaching adulthood without the psychological scars that most of us need to deal with before we can enjoy the fruits of the individuation process or spiritual development. We also thank you for the sense of liberation we now enjoy, knowing that the unintentional hurts we cause Joshua can be cleared without permanent damage!

A father realizes he was almost abusive.

I wish that I had read *The Aware Baby* before my daughter was born. I hadn't realized that I really was constantly distracting my baby when she was crying by gently rocking and cooing. I've wept heavily reading parts of this book. Both my daughter and I experienced very extreme distress at times when I could just not stop her from crying. It made me feel so useless at a time when I felt that I had to prove that I was okay as a parent (mostly to my daughter's mother). I wish that someone had told me that it was actually very, very important that she do some very hard crying. On two occasions I shook her so hard in anger and frustration over her crying that (I later found out) I might actually have killed her.

A mother would have been abusive.

I'm *finally* writing to you. I've wanted to since I found *The Aware Baby* a short nine months ago. Your book saved our lives. I really believe I would have become abusive without it. My daughter, Sandra, was only ten weeks old, but having come from an abusive, dysfunctional family myself, I was floundering and could not find answers that worked for us. After reading your book, I now have a happy, flourishing eleven-month-old daughter who I understand and adore. Thank you!! Mere words cannot express how much your books have enriched my life, my daughter's, and my husband's forever.

A crying baby opens up a mother's spiritual life.

I have been meaning to write to you with the purpose of sharing some of my experiences with my seven-month-old daughter, Linda, and, above all, thanking you for your book, *The Aware Baby*, which came into my hands when Linda was just six weeks old.

At that time she was beginning to have crying spells which I did not understand, and I was beginning to get frantic. Perhaps some of this crying was due to colic. I went off dairy products and the cramped, painful crying practically disappeared. On the other hand, at the time that I started reading your book, I was offering her my breast every time she cried, or walking her to sleep. She was nursing fitfully every hour or so during the day, and I was beginning to notice that she seemed kind of "zoned out."

The first week when I encouraged her to cry was really rough. For the first three days she did almost nothing but cry, and my family went around holding their ears and trying not to interfere. Just as I was losing my nerve, my family became supportive. Now I am the proud Mama of a seven-month-old baby who everyone says is so alert.

My work with Linda has opened up my spiritual life, and everywhere I am seeing affirmation of your ideas. I am so excited about the whole thing, I think it's terrific. And I feel you are on the cutting edge of a revolution that will be a change for the better. However, my cautious, conservative side wonders where it will take us. As I write this, I suspect that this is wrapped up in my own hesitation to begin crying.

My daughter is so alert and happy. I am so proud of her, and I think she will grow up to be a powerful adult. Perhaps, as she won't be carrying so much past hurt around with her, she will always be in touch with the person she is now: so close to whatever it is that's on the other side of existence, so fresh, so intelligent.

A ten-month-old boy sleeps through the night.

Your book, *The Aware Baby*, made its way to our home at the perfect time. I was an over-nurser and very much a control pattern for my infant son. After reading two chapters last week, I put your suggestions to work immediately. Richard welcomed the opportunity to cry, and then slept through the night for the first time ever! (He is ten months old.) The next day he cried heartily again and then fell asleep for two-and-a-half hours in his crib! What is remarkable is that he was used to sleeping in my arms and would always cry when put down either in his crib or in our bed, and would sleep only if I held him.

I've gotten to know him so much better and differently. Our bond has truly deepened since sharing these crying times together. I am so "in love" with him! I sense that he cries much clearer now, and he is much more expressive and communicative with me. He knows I really understand and accept his feelings, so he's much more open.

My husband and I have been undergoing severe marital stress. I have been reaching out to others in an effort to heal my pain and hurts. In between my therapy sessions, I keep talking to myself and letting the tears flow.

My husband has so much unacknowledged pain within, that he absolutely cannot tolerate crying in anyone else. He has refused to participate in your suggested exercises, and bans the baby and me to another room to do our crying. This is very hard for me to deal with, but I do, because he is a very loving, kind, generous and thoughtful man.

An aggressive ten-month-old boy begins to relax.

I have a ten-month-old boy who, up until one week ago, seemed quite distressed, yet cried very little. Ever since he was born, he has been a very active, squirming, kicking baby, and very strong. I interpreted this activity as his desire not to be held, especially since he always stopped crying when I put him down. He grew very fast and strong, and seemed to be developing perfectly except for the fact that he didn't like to be held and could not be comforted from his continual whining. He also began biting me and pulling my hair very hard. I tried to accept him the way he was, yet had feelings of grief and anger at his seeming rejection of me.

Then I found your book, *The Aware Baby*. I got rid of his pacifier immediately and began holding him when he cried. It was (and continues to be) very painful, emotionally, to hold him because he attempts everything to kick and squirm his way out of my arms. But, he does cry and does eventually look into my eyes, and his body does eventually relax. The joy in holding him after a crying time is so fulfilling and joyful, I can't tell you. He is, as you describe, more relaxed and happier. I feel as if, after ten months, I finally have my baby.

A one-year-old girl becomes cuddly.

Before I read *The Aware Baby*, I was caught in a dilemma: how to deal with a crying baby with no apparent reason for pain or need. Should a mother nurse her baby or let her cry it out? I wasn't comfortable with leaving my baby to cry in her crib so I tried to comfort her with nursing. So at one year of age, my daughter was a darling, sweet, "good" baby, but she nursed constantly, was overweight, and I was an irritable, angry, frustrated parent with very sore nipples. I dreaded nursing because my daughter wanted me constantly, but would squirm, arch her back, scratch and cry. I also hated bedtime. I hated leaving her in her bed to "cry it out," but found no alternative. When she cried I had tried to nurse, or distract or comfort her. When I failed and she screamed, I became frustrated and rageful. My back "went out" and I developed arthritis in my hands. The situation got so bad that I started yelling "shut up." As our relationship deteriorated, I sought help from our local child abuse prevention agency. They helped me to deal with my own feelings of rage and inadequacy. But I never could figure out *why* her crying "pushed by button" to the degree that it did. I learned how to deal with her "misbehavior," but couldn't figure out the underlying causes, until I read *The Aware Baby*.

Clearly, I didn't understand her crying. I thought she was trying to communicate, "Mother, *do something*!" In fact, she was trying to heal herself. I no longer felt that I had to "do something" (which, when it failed, made me feel like failure). I could simply sit back and "actively let her cry." No longer did I have to dump her in her crib and let her scream. Now, whenever she was fussy or "misbehaved," I could calmly take her to her room and just hold her. I could put up my feet and get a rest myself. It *is* very difficult work, holding a screaming, back-arching, raging child. But after about 40 minutes she begins to look around the room, play with my hair, and is a different person. Sometimes she falls asleep peacefully in my arms or she gets down to play happily for hours.

She is now a different person. She is cuddly. (She never before let me hold her, even as an infant. I never got the positive feedback that I needed to know that I was parenting effectively.) Now she only nurses a few times a day (sometimes I have to encourage her for nutritional reasons). I no longer dread those long evening hours leading up to bedtime. Now she plays happily until around 9 p.m., and then snuggles with me in bed until she falls asleep.

I am now a different parent. I have an understanding of a profound need that we all have, and I feel that I am helping her to become a happy and healthy person. Thank you Dr. Solter.

A two-year-old boy rages and sleeps through the night.

Thank you so much for your two books, *The Aware Baby* and *Helping Young Children Flourish*. They have been very helpful in understanding what is going on between myself and my child.

After reading your books I was certain I had over-nursed my baby for the past two years. He was a very plump baby with rolls of fat.

People used to make remarks to me that he was fat and always had a "boob" in his mouth. I felt I was supplying all his needs by nursing on demand. I knew that every time Robert fed he wasn't hungry, but that perhaps he just needed the security, and that was my role as a mother to supply that. Also, I wanted to compensate for me not being breast-fed as a baby, and being left to cry it out. Robert has always slept with us and been nursed to sleep, waking up two to four times a night for the past year or so.

So when I read that he was using nursing as a control pattern, I decided to stop nursing him to sleep at nighttime, to start with. On my first attempt, I held him and let him rage for about 15 minutes. My husband stomped off and said I was torturing him, because that's what it sounded like. I felt dreadful and wondered if I was doing the right thing. I tried to reason that this was benefitting him and allowing him to release tensions. But he just seemed to be overheating and getting more and more upset with me. After some time I gave him the breast to calm him down, and he went into a very deep sleep for several hours.

Last night I let him rage again for 30 minutes, and was surprised at the anger he displayed. He would struggle against me holding him, then want me to hold him, then reject me and want his Papa. All this has brought up deep hurts and emotions for me, so I have decided to do some Primal Therapy. He eventually stopped crying when I got him to understand he could have the breast in the morning. He then slept through the night (waking only once, but putting himself back to sleep without going on the breast)! I want to continue doing this every night now, although I find it very hard to do.

A three-year-old girl expresses jealousy.

Your book, *The Aware Baby* made the single biggest difference for me as a new mother!! It was so helpful, so realistic and practical, as well as so affirming for parent and child! Even though my daughter is now almost three years old, I still use your books as my bible. (I've also bought your second book.) Through the endless maze of parenting advice, books, and articles, your philosophy and book shone through as a beacon of white light, awareness, and knowledge. It was the only thing that made sense to me and had practical applications with successful results.

I've just had a second child who is now four weeks old, and Elizabeth (my three-year-old) is going through fairly intense sibling rivalry. When I try to spend time with Elizabeth to let her rage and cry her jealous feelings out, holding and nurturing her, the new baby starts crying! If I go to the baby to check on why she's crying, Elizabeth feels abandoned and even more jealous! I feel so confused and torn. Helping my children release their feelings while holding and comforting them is so important to them, but I can't seem to do it effectively with two children needing me at the same time!

(See the following section on the most commonly asked questions for a response to this problem.)

A mother understands her four-year-old daughter better.

Coming across your books has been an absolute God-send to me. I am so thankful that you wrote them because they are changing my life.

My daughter is four years old and seemed to be whiny and clingy too much of the time. Your book opened my eyes to how exactly I had instituted control patterns when she was an infant, and how these became second nature as she grew older. Because I got the idea from a breast-feeding support group that I could use nursing to comfort her, and because I could not bear to hear her cry, I mainly used nursing in the beginning to keep her from letting go of her feelings (although at the time I didn't know that, and thought I was doing the right thing).

When my daughter was around three-and-a-half, I began going to 12-step meetings (Adult Children of Alcoholics, specifically), and began releasing my feelings and working through the wreckage of my own warped attitudes and behavior. A lot of anger came out and was mostly directed at my daughter even though it had little or nothing to do with her. I became desperate to find help, and wanted to change my behavior so badly. Well, crying through many avenues has helped the anger subside. Your books and the concrete help they offer make me breathe a sigh of relief.

Not only can I see all the things my daughter uses to avoid her feelings, but I can see how my own control patterns began. It feels so good to know that any damage I've done can be healed if I allow her to do the crying she needs. Thank you so much for bringing all this to light.

A five-year-old girl catches up on her crying.

When Mary was born (five years ago), she nursed for one hour at a stretch or more. My in-laws said, "You'll get sore breasts," "Get a pacifier." So I was relieved when, at about 11 weeks, Mary found her thumb and the burden of extended sucking passed from me!

As I was reading your description of control patterns in *The Aware Baby,* including breast-feeding...what!!! breast-feeding a control pattern? I was slightly upset and should have realized that I'd gotten into something valuable for me. But unfortunately, I'm a bit thick, and need at least some predisposition to new material in order to be able to grasp it. So when I read *Helping Young Children Flourish* last month, it suddenly came all clear to me in your first chapter. Eureka! If, in those first 11 weeks, I had refused the breast (appropriately) in order to support the tears that would have followed, Mary would probably not be such an intense five-year-old.

As far as now letting Mary learn to cry instead of suck her thumb (her main and beloved control pattern), I really feel unsure of how to proceed. But I would have to say I saw some progress almost from the moment I started. When she starts to cry, sometimes I see her thumb reflexively heading for her mouth, and frequently she decides not to put it in, in favor of crying. And at the end, when the raging finally has stopped, she is so fresh and clear, it is as if the event didn't happen or had no weight. Sometimes she even picks up the stuff she threw, totally matter-of-factly.

I feel like I have no notion yet of how much to hold her and how much to leave her alone when she requests it with words. I remember as a child screaming and punching to be left alone *while wanting with all my heart to be held and supported and loved.* Mostly I continue holding, and when I don't, I check in rather frequently to see how it's all going. I assume this poor girl has a lot of backlog crying to do.

5. THE MOST COMMONLY ASKED QUESTIONS

This section contains the questions most commonly asked by parents and teachers who come to my workshops and who consult with me privately.

I agree that it's good for children to cry, but I don't want them to do it near me. Is it okay to tell them to cry somewhere else?

I realize that it's not easy to be with a crying child, but it is important to remember that our own childhood experiences affect our responses to children. We would not find it nearly so difficult to accept children's emotional expressions if we ourselves had been allowed to cry and rage as children with an adult's loving attention.

Everyone has a right to peace and quiet, and you should make sure you get enough time away from children, whether you are a parent or a teacher. But when children are in our care, are we justified in ignoring their genuine needs for attention simply because we feel uncomfortable?

There is a tendency, especially in the United States, to force children into independence. One of the ways this is manifested is in the popular discipline method commonly known as "time-out." The child is asked to sit on a chair away from other people, or is sent to another room. This approach is based on the behaviorist notion that disagreeable behaviors will disappear when they are not rewarded with adult attention. I have written extensively about the hidden pitfalls of this form of discipline.[1]

There are several reasons why I do not recommend isolation or withdrawal of attention from children who are crying or raging. First, children experience this as a form of punishment. They cannot help but feel that they are doing something wrong, that they are being "bad" for crying. This withdrawal of love and attention at a time when they need it the most will lower their self-esteem, because a part of themselves (the need to release strong emotions) has been rejected. Children need unconditional love and acceptance, not conditional attention based on how they are feeling.

Secondly, isolation and withdrawal of love can produce more painful feelings in children that will only increase the need for further crying. A child who is sent to another room may feel confused, insecure, anxious, frustrated, angry and resentful. If a child is asked to sit alone in a chair separate from a group of children, she may end up feeling embarrassed and ashamed.

Thirdly, this form of discipline is not a useful role model for adult relationships. Do we want our children to tell their future co-workers or spouses to go to another room when upset and come out only when they can "behave themselves?" Rather than teach children to break off communication with others, it makes more sense to demonstrate good listening, so that our children can learn this valuable skill for use later in life.

Fourthly, children who are sent to another room, or told to sit quietly on a chair when they cry, may eventually learn to suppress their tears. Children release feelings much more effectively and completely when an adult accepts and acknowledges their pain. Anything that inhibits this healthy release is a disservice to children, because it increases their susceptibility to a variety of emotional and physical problems.

Finally, my greatest concern about ignoring crying or raging children is what this does to the parent/child relationship. As the mother of two children who are almost grown up, I know that it is vitally important to keep communication open as children grow older. If we refuse to listen to children's feelings when they are little, pushing them away from us because we don't like the sound of their crying, how can we possibly expect them, as teenagers, to come to us with their problems? They will soon learn to push *us* away because they have learned that we refuse to listen. They will search elsewhere for the unconditional love and acceptance that they are not receiving at home. Don't forget that, in a few short years, your children will become adolescents, and how you treat them now has an impact on your future relationship with them.

Don't children sometimes cry just to manipulate their parents? If I reinforce this, won't they cry more to get my attention?

When no immediate need is obvious, and children use crying as a stress-release mechanism, it is easy to attribute the crying to some inner need to dominate or manipulate the parents. This misunderstanding is especially likely to occur when children use small pretexts to cry or become excessively demanding because of a build-up of stress (the "broken-cookie" phenomenon).

There is a mistaken notion that children can produce tears at will, and that not all tears are "genuine." This is incorrect. Children cannot fake crying. If there are tears, a healthy release is taking place, even though the cause for the crying may not be apparent. Professional actors learn to produce real tears on stage by recalling a traumatic childhood experience and letting themselves feel the pain. The crying is genuine.

So even though some children can turn their crying on and off at will (depending on how safe they feel), this does not mean that the crying is fake or that they are trying to "manipulate" their parents. When children have cried enough, there are no more tears, and no amount of attention can cause children to cry more than they need to. It is important to remember that *children cry when they feel safe enough to do so*, but that they cry only as much as needed to release tensions.

It helps to think of crying and raging as processes similar to defecating. The need to cry gradually builds up and eventually finds an outlet in a crying session or temper tantrum. This is comparable to the need to defecate, which builds up until the urge for release is felt. We don't accuse children of manipulating us when they defecate! And we don't worry about causing diarrhea by paying attention to children when they sit on the potty! We know that there is a finite amount of feces, and the child cannot produce more at will just to get our attention.

It is easy to misinterpret children's motivations based on our own emotions. If you frequently feel manipulated when your child cries, I recommend that you explore your childhood memories. If you were made to feel powerless as a child, and your behavior controlled by punishments or rewards, it is only natural for you to dislike and resist anything that resembles an attempt to control or manipulate you (even if it is not).

This issue is further complicated by the notion of "spoiling," which did not exist until the industrial revolution. After that time, extended families were broken up for the first time in the history of the human species. Society became more mobile, and people went to live where the jobs were. This resulted in overburdened parents with no nearby support system of grandparents, aunts, uncles, cousins and siblings. Child-rearing methods changed drastically from the previous indulgent style of parenting.

Mothers were warned not to spoil or indulge their children, but to push them toward independence. This led to the deplorable practices of early weaning, early toilet-training (sometimes as early as three weeks of age), forcing babies to sleep alone, strict scheduled feedings, ignoring babies when they cried, and punitive discipline. (Punitive discipline was not new for older children, but became extended into infancy.) The feeling of being manipulated by a child's crying probably originated along with the fear of spoiling.

So the fact that you *feel* manipulated by your child's crying does not imply that your child's *intention* is to manipulate you.

How can I distinguish genuine needs from unreasonable demands?

In the section about the "broken-cookie" phenomenon (Part III, Section 3), I describe how children make use of little pretexts to cry about accumulated stress in their lives. Sometimes they become overly demanding. Setting a firm limit is often sufficient to trigger the flow of tears. How can one know for sure what a child really needs? There is no simple answer to this question.

Here is a situation described by a mother who attended one of my workshops. Her four-year-old daughter wanted to wear the same pair of underpants every day, because it had her favorite cartoon characters on it. If these underpants were not available (because they were dirty and had not yet been laundered), she had a temper tantrum. Her mother was therefore in the habit of washing this pair of underpants every evening so that her daughter could wear them each day. The mother's question at my workshop was whether I thought that this was a real need or a "broken-cookie" phenomenon. In other words, when her daughter had a temper tantrum about this, was it really about the underpants or was it about other, unrelated stress?

In a situation like this, I recommend, first, discussing the issue and doing conflict-resolution with the child at a time when nobody is upset about it. The mother can say, "We have a problem. You want to wear these same underpants every day, and I am tired of washing them every day. What can we do about this?" Together, they can think of possible solutions. One idea could be to buy more underpants with the same cartoon characters. If they can find a mutually agreeable solution to this conflict, the problem will be solved. In retrospect, the mother will realize that it was very important to her daughter to wear those underpants.

However, if no solution can be found that works, this is an indication that the underlying issue probably has nothing to do with the underpants. The child is simply using that as a pretext to do some crying. Or perhaps the problem will be solved with no more tantrums, but the girl will then find another pretext to have a temper tantrum in the mornings. Perhaps, all of a sudden, her socks are the wrong color, or her shoes feel uncomfortable.

Here is an example of a situation with my daughter when the need was not a genuine one:

> When my daughter was seven years old, she began to cry every morning about the toe seams in her socks that bothered her. So I bought socks for her without seams at the toes. However, this did not solve the morning crying. It seemed as if she found something to cry about almost every morning while getting dressed for school. This occurred during a period of a few months when two other girls at school, who had formerly been her close friends, were excluding her from their play. It was her way of releasing stress resulting from a difficult social situation.

How do you expect me to accept crying when I have more than one child to take care of? Isn't this approach unrealistic?

Meeting the emotional needs of more than one child is a challenge, whether you are the parent of children close together in age, or a caretaker with several babies or young children. Parents of twins have an especially difficult job.

You must understand that you are not going to be able to meet all the children's needs all the time. If more than one child is crying, you can decide who needs attention first. A general guideline is to give the youngest child as much physical contact and attention as possible. Give the older ones support and attention through smiling, reassuring talk, and an occasional hug or pat (if you have a free hand). Children who observe your loving response when another child cries or rages may feel jealous, but they will receive some reassurance from being in an environment that accepts the expression of strong emotions.

Parenting and working with young children are extremely demanding jobs. We must realize, however, that it is not natural to be caring for children in groups, or to have the sole responsibility of more than one child under the age of three years for any length of time. Group care for babies and toddlers is very different from the natural environment in which our species evolved.

During hundreds of thousands of years of human prehistory, our ancestors were hunters and gatherers living in extended family groups. There were always more adults than children in these clans, and no single adult had the sole responsibility for babies and young children. Parenting was a shared responsibility. Furthermore, studies of modern hunter-gatherer societies have revealed that the children in each family are born about three years apart on the average. Each child receives considerable individual attention during the first few years. Our genetic make-up has not changed since the hunter-gatherer stage. It seems that children under three years of age, therefore, have a built-in expectation for individual attention.[2]

Given the current cultural and economic situation in industrialized countries, infants and toddlers under age three are being cared for increasingly in group settings. This is not ideal, but it is a reality that we must make the best of. My advice for daycare directors is to have small child/adult ratios, as little staff turnover as possible, and individualized feeding and sleeping schedules for the children. Perhaps most importantly, try to encourage the formation of strong attachments between children and teachers. Strive for an environment that reduces stress, but that accepts tears and tantrums.

Teachers can be especially helpful in giving emotional support and acceptance of crying if the parents are unable or unwilling to do so, or if there is a stressful home situation. Teachers can play a crucial role in crises such as parental divorce. Children cry wherever they feel safe enough to do so. If they feel safe at home, they will do most of their crying there. However, if they are punished or ignored for crying at home, or if the parents themselves are a major source of pain, the children will attempt to do their crying with other caretakers. Whenever a child cries with you, whether you are the parent or another caretaker, you can feel honored that the child trusts you enough to release feelings in your presence. It is a tribute to your good attention and care.

Don't children need to learn to adjust to society?

Yes, children do need to learn when and where it is appropriate to cry (just as they need to learn toilet etiquette). But this is too much to expect of a child under five years of age (and sometimes older). Children's feelings are very intense and immediate. They find it exceedingly difficult to hold them in and save them up for more appropriate times.

Parents generally try to make sure that babies wear fresh diapers before going out, and that toilet-trained children use the toilet before leaving the home. You can take similar precautions with crying and raging. Let your children complete any needed crying before you go out. If you see that a temper tantrum is brewing, try to wait until it has occurred. This is not always possible, of course, and even with the best of precautions, your child may need to cry or have a temper tantrum in a public place.

These emotional outbursts do not usually bother other people as much as parents fear, and they provide you with an excellent opportunity to demonstrate aware listening and acceptance of feelings. However, if your child starts to fuss in a place of worship, library, restaurant, concert hall, or anywhere else that people are likely to be disturbed, it is wise to take your child to another place. If she needs to cry, you can stay with her while she releases feelings. If it is not possible to take your child out, you can try to stop the crying with distractions. You should realize, however, that you are probably only postponing it until a more appropriate time. (It is unrealistic to expect infants and young children to be quiet for long periods of time in the places mentioned above.)

My child sucks his thumb and doesn't cry much. What can I do?

When children repeatedly stop themselves from crying through control patterns such as thumb sucking, the parents are sometimes very concerned, and wonder how to stop these habits.

I consider all repetitive and prolonged thumb sucking to be a control pattern (as opposed to the occasional exploratory act of putting a thumb or fingers in the mouth). Babies and children who suck their thumbs are repressing their feelings in this manner, just as an adult might smoke a cigarette when feeling upset or tense. In the latter case, however, the physiological addiction to nicotine is also a part of the control pattern. Children suck their thumbs when they are experiencing stress or painful emotions, and are not feeling quite safe enough to cry.

Some babies suck their thumbs before they are born. However, most thumb sucking starts during the first six months. It is usually a baby's response to a parent's repeated (but well-intentioned) attempts to distract or "soothe" the crying, in hopes of making the baby feel better. Thumb sucking can also result from being ignored during crying spells.

Prolonged thumb sucking can result in displacement of the teeth and the need for orthodontia later on. It can also turn into a nail biting or smoking habit. However, thumb sucking does not imply that a child has deep psychological problems or will grow up to be a troubled adult. It certainly does *not* mean that you have failed as a parent. I think of thumb sucking as a little habit that children develop, indicating that some painful feelings are being held back. Usually, it is not difficult to help children overcome this habit.

It is advisable for parents to look for ways to reduce thumb sucking, because it is better for children to release feelings than hold them in. Commenting on it or using verbal reminders will not be helpful, nor is it necessary to pull the child's thumb out of her mouth. The most effective approach is to focus on making the child feel safe enough so that she no longer needs to repress her feelings in this manner. (See the guidelines for creating emotional safety in Part IV, Section 2).

It is helpful to accept any crying or raging that occurs spontaneously and try to refrain from distracting your child during these outbursts. Accidents involving minor physical injuries provide excellent opportunities for you to encourage a thumb sucker's crying. After bumps and bruises, these children will often cry for at least a short time before putting their thumb in their mouth. You can give your child full attention at these times and encourage the crying. It may be helpful to say, "It really hurts, doesn't it?" or "It's okay to cry." You can gently touch the injured part of your child's body in order to draw her attention back to the pain. The child may make use of the opportunity of a minor injury to release non-related emotions. In this manner, the child will gradually develop feelings of greater safety and trust.

The use of touching and closeness can be very effective with thumb suckers. When your child sucks his thumb, give him attention, hold him, touch him, make eye contact, talk to him, and try to draw his attention out. If necessary, you can gently touch the hand that is at his mouth to help him realize that he is sucking his thumb (but without mentioning it). With an infant, it can be extremely effective to caress the baby's forehead or cheek while focusing full attention on her. (See the example on page 72.) When children feel that another person is really present with them, they will spontaneously take their thumb out of their mouth to cry.

If your thumb sucking toddler or older child resists your closeness, you can be cheerfully affectionate and persist in following her even if she walks away from you. Reassure your child that you really do want to be with her. Do not be surprised and do not take it personally if your child shows anger directed at you. In response to your focused attention, a verbal child may start crying and blame you for making her feel bad. Don't worry, she's just catching up on her crying and using you as a sounding board!

Another helpful intervention with thumb suckers is to encourage laughter. With infants who suck their thumbs, you can engage them in a game of peek-a-boo (from the age of six months on). With older children, you can suggest silly games in which you pretend to be weak, ignorant, scared, or stupid. Let them "knock" you over. These activities will almost certainly cause children to take their thumb out of their mouth in order to laugh, and the laughter will help them release tensions and accumulated feelings of anxiety, anger, or powerlessness. This kind of play will also help contribute to the bonding and trust between you and your child. It helps create the emotional safety that your child needs in order to bring up deeper feelings and cry.

Is it wrong to comfort a baby with breast-feeding?

It is important to be aware of babies' real needs in each situation. There is much confusion about food, sucking, and feelings, and it is all too easy to misinterpret babies' needs. If you yourself overeat or smoke when you are upset, this is going to be a difficult issue for you to figure out.

In a study of mothers' interpretation of infant crying, three kinds of crying were recorded (pain, hunger, and startle) and played back to the mothers. They incorrectly perceived too many of the samples as hunger cries.[3] This common misinterpretation of crying would partly explain the tendency of many mothers to over-nurse their infants.

Babies do need a loving mother who fills their needs for food and closeness, and breast-feeding is the ideal way to meet both of these needs. But babies also need parents who can listen to them release feelings, and it is important to establish a genuine listening relationship right from the start. As stated repeatedly in this book, babies should never be left alone when they are crying. But crying while being held and loved can provide babies with the opportunity for a healthy release of tensions.

It is easy to fall into the "nurse-the-baby, all-is-well" trap, because babies at the breast appear to be content. They cannot cry and nurse at the same time. However, not all fussiness indicates hunger, and all too often nursing serves to repress the crying, at least temporarily. Mothers are led to believe that nursing is an acceptable way to comfort babies even when they are not hungry. I think this attitude is so prevalent because many people do not recognize the intensity of infant emotional pain, or understand the processes of emotional release.

It is important to realize that the rooting and sucking reflexes (turning their heads and sucking anything that touches their cheeks) are strong, automatic reflexes in babies during the first few months. Babies will suck automatically. This wired-in reflex is necessary for survival. During the millions of years of evolution, babies who did not have this strong tendency to suck would not have survived. This means, however, that during the first few weeks babies do not choose to begin nursing any more than you choose to kick your leg following a tap on your knee (the knee-jerk reflex).

If a mother repeatedly offers the breast at times when the baby is attempting to release stress through crying, nursing can become a habit and turn into a control pattern. After the reflexes disappear and nursing comes under voluntary control by infants, it may seem as if babies want to nurse when they are not hungry but only upset. (See pages 68 to 69 for guidelines on how frequently infants need to nurse.)

What about whining?

Whining is generally caused by a need to cry that hasn't yet been fulfilled. Whining is attempted, but unsuccessful, crying. Some parents find whining to be more irritating than a full-blown cry, especially when it goes on all day long.

There are several reasons that children whine. Perhaps they don't feel safe enough to have a full-blown cry, because they are afraid of being punished or reprimanded. Another possibility is that the child is feeling some painful feelings, but has not accumulated enough stress to trigger a full-blown cry.

At eight years of age, my son made an interesting comparison. (We used the word "sads" for the concept of sad feelings.) He said, "Sads are sort of like a bowl of sugar. There has to be a certain amount in there before you can take some out. When there's only a few crumbs at the bottom you can't get them out." He meant that he couldn't seem to have a good cry unless there was enough to cry about.

Sometimes children begin whining when adults have been too concerned about satisfying every little whim, inadvertently preventing a full-blown cry. Whiners may be looking for a pretext (such as a broken cookie) in order to get started crying. Sometimes you just have to wait until they find a pretext. Perhaps you can help by providing a firm limit (but without using punishment) if they are becoming unreasonably demanding or if their behavior is obnoxious.

Whining and clinging can be indications of physical pain or illness, so be sure to check that possibility. It is sometimes a child's way of saying that he is not feeling well.

When I use holding, how do I know that I'm not creating a new frustration for my child?

Holding a hyperactive, obnoxious, or violent child in order to stop his behavior and to promote crying should be done with awareness and sensitivity. *It should never be done in the spirit of anger or punishment.* If you are so angry at your child that you have an urge to harm her, it is advisable to postpone holding and take some time out for yourself until you have regained a sense of composure. Holding your child in a spirit of anger will not provide her with the sense of security she needs, and it could also cause new anxiety or frustrations for her.

Before using holding, it is important to do all you can to create emotional safety for the child (as described Part IV, Section 2). Once you have a good relationship with the child, I recommend using holding primarily for the times when the child is violent or extremely obnoxious, and cannot seem to reach the point of crying without some assistance. Holding can also be useful when the child is clearly showing, by her whining and clinging behavior, that she needs to cry and wants to be held.

If the child is acting obnoxiously or violently, first you need to assess the situation to see if she is reacting in a legitimate way against some hurtful behavior from adults. Is she being expected to do something unnecessary against her wish? Is she reacting to authoritarian discipline? Is she being shown lack of respect? Are her needs being ignored? Holding a child in these cases will only create further frustration for her.

If you are fairly certain that an accumulation of pent-up stress is the underlying cause of the obnoxious or violent behavior, you can use holding as a strategy to help the child release her painful feelings. Be loving but firm. Gather her in your arms, even though she may protest vehemently by hitting, kicking, or yelling. Persist lovingly in maintaining close contact during this initial resistance, while protecting yourself against her attempts to hurt you. Be sure to give her some room to move. After children can talk, they sometimes protest by demanding things they don't really need, claiming you are hurting them, yelling that they hate you, and so on. Reassure your child that you love her, and explain that you are going to hold her for a little while to keep her from hurting anyone. Explain that you need to keep everyone safe.

Children who need to cry usually begin doing so within a minute or two of being held like this. Some children continue to fight and struggle even after the crying begins. If your child is still struggling to get away after five minutes, I recommend letting her push her way out of your arms, and then observing her behavior. If she resumes her obnoxious or violent behavior, or seeks attention by whining and clinging to you, hold her again to help her release more tears.

If your child does not begin crying after a few minutes, but continues to protest verbally, and to hit or kick you, this is an indication that she is not feeling safe enough to cry. There is no point in continuing with the holding in this case, because it will only frustrate both of you.

If your child becomes calm but withdrawn into herself and doesn't cry or make eye contact with you, the holding is not effective in allowing the needed tears. You can try changing the position. Children who have a nursing control pattern do not cry easily when they are in the standard nursing position with their mother. Holding them in another position can help them begin the crying they need to do.

Be prepared for long crying sessions. Holding can help children release very early trauma, such as that caused prenatally and during the birth process, and the emotional release can be very intense. If your child is calm, relaxed, happy, and loving after crying, the holding was effective. If your child's behavior does not improve after crying, perhaps she needs another kind of attention besides holding. Most parents notice a dramatic improvement in children's mood and behavior after holding sessions.

After the age of seven or eight years, children are less in need of the physical restraint and reassurance provided by holding. As they grow older, they are better able to control their violent impulses, and they can also make better use of other pretexts when they need to cry. Language is processed more meaningfully by older children, and a verbal limit (such as a firm but loving "No!") can be as effective as holding in helping an older child make the transition from obnoxious or aggressive behavior to healing tears.

I agree that it is important for children to cry, but my spouse (or mother-in-law, baby-sitter, teacher, etc.) tries to stop my child from crying. What can I do about this?

This is a cause of concern for many parents. First of all, don't try to give these people information about crying while your child is crying. This almost never works, because the people are usually too upset by the crying to listen to what you have to say. Instead, choose a time when everybody is happy and relaxed, preferably away from the children, and then calmly share your approach. An attitude conveying, "This is what works for me and seems to help my child," is generally more effective than a confrontation that opposes the "right way" against the "wrong way" to respond to a crying child. When you give people a chance to talk about their own childhoods, they become more aware of the harmful consequences of trying to stop the processes of emotional release. Perhaps the other person would be willing to read an article or a book about crying (such as this one).

Some people have had their crying so repressed that they cannot understand this approach, no matter how many times you discuss this with them. If you think a person's attitude is harmful, you have the right to restrict contact with your child. Keep in mind, however, that it is good for children to learn to adapt to all kinds of people, and it is not always necessary to protect them from other people, except in cases of abuse.

Children learn to save up their crying for the people with whom they feel the safest. If Grandma cannot stand to hear your son cry, he will probably save his crying for times when he is not with her. He can still have a loving and meaningful relationship with his grandmother. Maybe she has more patience than anyone else for answering his incessant questions, or for reading the same book to him over and over again. Everybody has certain strengths and weaknesses in relating to children, and children learn quickly how to benefit from each person's strengths.

Children can learn to handle relationships with other people surprisingly well, even if these people cannot support their strong emotions, provided the children have opportunities to vent their feelings with *somebody*. It is best if they have contact with a good, supportive listener on a daily basis, at least until the age of six or seven years. After that, they can save up their feelings for longer periods.

6. SUPPORTING PARENTS OF CHILDREN WHO CRY

If you work with parents, or have contact with them as a professional, it is important to be supportive of those whose children cry a lot. As stated at the beginning of this book, 80 percent of abusive parents admitted that crying was the factor that triggered their violent acts. Be especially supportive of parents whose babies had difficult births or prenatal distress, because those are the babies more likely to be fussy and difficult to care for.

Parents can benefit from four specific kinds of help and support. First, they may need suggestions for ways to reduce stress in their children's lives, so the children will have less to cry about. However, even though parents are sometimes the cause of children's emotional pain, *never blame parents directly for their children's crying.* Parents need reassurance that the crying does not mean they are inadequate.

Secondly, parents need correct information about crying, and reminders that it is beneficial for their children. They need to know that their child is not rejecting or manipulating them. You can encourage parents to hold their crying babies (and young children), and accept the crying rather than punish, distract, or ignore their children at those times.

Thirdly, the parents themselves need to be listened to and allowed to express their own strong emotions that are triggered by their child's crying, specifically feelings of anger, anxiety, guilt, and powerlessness. They also need opportunities to talk about their own childhoods, and how they were treated when they cried as children.

Finally, parents of babies and children who cry a lot need an occasional respite from parenting responsibilities. One or two hours away from their children can make a huge difference in helping parents gain renewed understanding and patience.

If there is severe stress in the child's life, you should refer the family to an appropriate helping agency. If you suspect child abuse, you are required by law in the United States to report this to a child protective agency. Be aware, however, that crying does not necessarily imply child abuse, although it does imply that the child is releasing stress. As stated above, however, crying can *lead to* physical abuse if the parents are having a hard time dealing with it and not getting enough support.

Physical abuse creates a vicious cycle because it causes more stress for the child, which creates a need for more crying, which in turn increases the likelihood of more abuse.

When parents are receiving adequate support and information about crying, I predict a dramatic reduction in physical child abuse. In fact, this may prove to be the most crucial factor needed in order to reduce this kind of violence.

Everybody can be supportive of parents when children cry. Sometimes a friendly comment is all that is needed. When I see an exasperated parent with a crying child in a public place, I try to make a supportive remark. I have found that the following comments help the parents relax and feel more accepting of their children: "It looks like you're both having a hard day." "What a beautiful baby (child) you have!" "It's hard when they cry, isn't it?" "I wish I could cry like that!" I once prevented a mother from spanking her three-year-old, raging son, simply by saying, "What a good crier he is! I bet he'll never get ulcers!"

Conclusion

When children are free to release the emotions resulting from trauma, loss, frustrations, and fears, their bodies and their minds will be free from the effects of stress and trauma. *The main message of this book is that emotional problems, behavioral problems, and stress-related illnesses are not caused by stress itself, but by the suppression of the natural healing mechanisms, specifically crying and raging, that serve the purpose of restoring the body's physiological and psychological balance following stress.*

Even in the best environment, with plenty of loving care, children's lives are not free from stress. Furthermore, unexpected traumatic events can occur anywhere and at any time. In spite of hardships and painful experiences, children can heal themselves from stress and trauma through the natural recovery processes of tears and tantrums. This will allow them to become emotionally healthy, eager and able to learn, compassionate, cooperative, and non-violent. If we can remember to trust these processes, human beings of any age can be healed. It is never too late to begin.

REFERENCES

The references below appear in the order in which they are cited. The numbers correspond to the small numbers in the text.

PART I: SOME FACTS ABOUT TEARS & TANTRUMS

1. INTRODUCTION: A HUGE MISUNDERSTANDING (pages 3 to 7)

1. Jones, S. (1983). *Crying Babies, Sleepless Nights*. New York: Warner.
2. Kitzinger, S. (1989). *The Crying Baby*. Viking.
3. Murray, A. (1979). Infant crying as an elicitor of parental behavior: An examination of two models. *Psychological Bulletin*, 86, 191-215.
   Frodi, A. (1985). When empathy fails: Aversive infant crying and child abuse. In B.M. Lester and C.F.Z. Boukydis (Eds.). *Infant Crying: Theoretical and Research Perspectives*. New York: Plenum Press.
4. Weston, J. (1968). The pathology of child abuse. In R. Helfer and C. Kempe (Eds.). *The Battered Child*. Chicago: University of Chicago Press.
5. Sulzer, J. (1748). *Versuch von der Erziehung und Unterweisung der Kinder (An Essay on the Education and Instruction of Children)*, quoted in Alice Miller (1984), *For Your Own Good: Hidden Cruelty in Child-rearing and the Roots of Violence*. New York: Farrar, Straus, Giroux.

2. STRESS-RELEASE MECHANISMS IN CHILDREN (pages 8 to 12)

1. Piaget, J. (1962). *Play, Dreams and Imitation in Childhood*. New York: W.W. Norton & Company, Inc.
2. Axline, V.M. (1969). *Play Therapy*. Ballantine Books.
   Oaklander, V. (1978). *Windows to Our Children*. The Gestalt Journal, P.O. Box 990, Highland, NY 12528.
   Schaefer, C.E. & O'Connor, K.J. (Eds.) (1983). *Handbook of Play Therapy. Vol. 1: Personality Processes*. New York: John Wiley & Sons.

Schaefer, C.E. & O'Connor, K.J. (Eds.) (1994). *Handbook of Play Therapy. Vol. 2: Advances and Innovations.* New York: John Wiley & Sons.

Landreth, G.L., Homeyer, L.E., Glover, G., & Sweeney. (1996). *Play Therapy Interventions With Children's Problems.* Jasson Aronson.

O'Connor, K. & Braverman, L.M. (Eds.) (1997). *Play Therapy and Practice: A Comparative Presentation.* New York: John Wiley & Sons.

3. Fry, W.F., Jr. (1992). The physiological effects of humor, mirth, and laughter. *Journal of the American Medical Association*, 267, 13, 1857-1858.

Hubert, W., Moller, M. & de Jong Meyer, R. (1993). Film induced amusement changes in saliva cortisol levels. *Psychoneuroendocrinology*, 18, 265-272.

Goodheart, A. (1994). *Laughter Therapy.* Santa Barbara, California: Less Stress Press.

4. Honig, A. (1986). Stress and coping in children. In J.B. McCracken (Ed.), *Reducing Stress in Young Children's Lives.* Washington, DC, NAEYC.

Greenberg, P. (1991). *Character Development: Encouraging Self-esteem and Self-discipline in infants, toddlers, and two-year-olds.* Washington, DC, NAEYC.

3. THE PHYSIOLOGY OF STRESS AND CRYING (pages 13 to 18)

1. Sapolsky, R.M. (1994). *Why Zebras Don't Get Ulcers: A Guide to Stress, Stress-Related Diseases, and Coping.* New York: W.H. Freeman & Company.

2. Van der Kolk, B.A. (1987). *Psychological Trauma.* Washington, DC: American Psychiatric Press.

3. Irwin, M., Daniels, M., Smith, T.L., Bloom, E., & Weiner, H. (1987). Impaired natural killer cell activity during bereavement. *Brain Behavior Immunology*, 1, 98-104.

4. Sapolsky, R.M. (1994). (See above)

5. Sapolsky, R.M. (1994). (See above)

6. Sapolsky, R.M. (1994). (See above)

7. Gross, J.J., Fredrickson, B.L., Levenson, R.W. (1994). The psychophysiology of crying. *Psychophysiology*, 31, 460-468.

8. Karle, W., Corriere, R., & Hart, J. (1973). Psychophysiological changes in abreaction therapy. Study I: Primal Therapy. *Psychotherapy*: Theory, Research and Practice, *10, 117-122.*

Woldenberg, L., Karle, W., Gold, S., Corriere, R., Hart, J., & Hopper, M. (1976). Psychophysiological changes in feeling therapy. *Psychological Reports*, 39, 1059-1062.

9. Frey II, W.H. & Langseth, M. (1985). *Crying: The Mystery of Tears.* Winston Press.
10. Frey II, W.H. & Langseth, M. (1985) (See above)
11. Van der Kolk, B.A. (1987). (See above)
12. Crepeau, M. T. (1980). A comparison of the behavior patterns and meanings of weeping among adult men and women across three health conditions (Doctoral dissertaion, University of Pittsburgh). *Dissertation Abstracts International*, 42, 137.
13. Siegel, B. (1986). *Love, Medicine, and Miracles.* New York: Harper & Row.
14. Doust, J.W.L. & Leigh, D. (1953). Studies in the physiology of awareness: The interrelations of emotions, life situations, and anoxemia in patients with bronchial asthma. *Psychosomatic Medicine*, 15, 292-311.
    Graham, O.T. & Wolf, S. (1950). Pathogenesis of urticaria. *Psychosomatic Medicine*, 13, 122.

4. THE PSYCHOLOGICAL BENEFITS OF CRYING (pages 19 to 25)

1. Breuer, J. & Freud, S. (1955). *Studies in Hysteria.* (translated by J. Strachey). London: The Hogarth Press.
2. Miller, A. (1984). *For Your Own Good: Hidden Cruelty in Child-Rearing and the Roots of Violence.* New York: Farrar, Straus, Giroux.
3. Pierce. R.A., Nichols, M.P., & DuBrin, J.R. (1983). *Emotional Expression in Psychotherapy.* New York: Gardner press.
4. Bergmann, T. *Children in the Hospital.* (1965). New York: International University Press.
5. Van der Kolk, B.A. (1987). *Psychological Trauma.* Washington, DC: American Psychiatric Press.
6. Bowlby, J. (1958). The Nature of the Child's Tie to His Mother. *International Journal of Psycho-Analysis*, 39, 350-373.
7. Bowlby, J. (1988). *A Secure Base.* Basic Books, Inc.
8. Walant, K. (1996). Fostering Healthy Attachment. *The Nurturing Parent.* (Summer 1996 issue).
9. Bowlby, J. (1988). (See above)

10. Bowlby, J. (1979). *The Making and Breaking of Affectional Bonds*. New York: Routledge.
11. Bowlby, J. (1988). (See above)
12. Van der Kolk, B.A. (1987). (See above)
13. Brown, B. & Rosenbaum, L. (1983). Stress effects on IQ. Paper presented at the meeting of the American Association for the Advancement of Science, Detroit.
14. Brownlee, S. U.S. (Nov. 11, 1996). *U.S. News and World Report*.
15. Sapolsky, R.M. (1994). *Why Zebras Don't Get Ulcers: A Guide to Stress, Stress-Related Diseases, and Coping*. New York: W.H. Freeman & Company.
16. Weissglass, J.(1997). *Ripples of Hope: Building Relationships for Educational Change*. Center for Educational Change in Mathematics and Science. University of California, Santa Barbara, California, 93115.

5. THE USE OF CRYING IN THERAPY WITH CHILDREN (pages 26 to 32)

1. Jewett, C. (1982). *Helping Children Cope With Separation and Loss*. Boston: Harvard Common Press.
2. Batchelor, E.S., Jr., Dean, R.S., Gray, J.W., & Wenck, S. (1991). Classification rates and relative risk factors for perinatal events predicting emotional/behavioral disorders in children. *Pre- and Perinatal Psychology Journal*, 5(4), 327-346.
3. Mednick, S.A. (1971). Birth defects and schozophrenia. *Psychology Today*, 4, 49.
   Roedding, J. (1991). Birth trauma and suicide: A study of the relationship between near-death experiences at birth and later suicidal behavior. *Pre- and Perinatal Psychology Journal*, 6(2), 145-167.
   Janov, A. (1983). *Imprints: The Lifelong Effects of the Birth Experience*. New York: Coward-McCann, Inc.
4. Emerson, W. (1989). Psychotherapy with infants and children. *Pre- and Perinatal Psychology Journal*, 3(3), 190-217.
   Emerson, W.R. & Schorr-Kon, S. (1993). Somatotropic Therapy. In *Innovative Therapies*. London: Open University Press.
5. Levine, P.A. (1997). *Waking the Tiger: Healing Trauma*. Berkeley: North Atlantic Books.
6. Waal, N. (1955). A special technique of psychotherapy with an autistic child. In F. Caplan (Ed.), *Emotional Problems of Early Childhood*. New York: Basic Books.

Zaslow, R.W. & Breger, L. (1969). A theory and treatment of autism. In L. Breger (Ed.), *Clinical-Cognitive Psychology: Models and Integrations*. New Jersey: Prentice-Hall.

Zaslow, R. & Menta, M. (1975). *The Psychology of the Z-process: Attachment and activity*. San Jose State University Press, California.

Welch, M.A. (1983). Retrieval from autism through mother-child holding therapy. In E.A. Tinbergen (Ed.). *Autistic Children: New Hope for a Cure*. London: George Allen & Unwin.

Prekop, J. (1983). Das Festhalten als Therapie bei Kindern mit Autismus-Syndrom. Anwendung der Therapie durch das "Festhalten" nach Welch/Tinbergen. Teil 1. (Holding as therapy for autistic children: Application of Welch/Tinbergen's holding therapy). Fruhforderung Interdisziplinar, Apr-Jun Vol. 2, No. 2, 54-64.

7. Magid, K. & McKelvey, C.A. (1987). *High Risk: Children Without a Conscience*. New York: Bantam Books.

Keck, G.C. & Kupecky, R.M. (1995). *Adopting the Hurt Child*. Pinon Press, Colorado Springs, CO.

8. Magid, K. & McKelvey, C.A. (1987). (See above)

Keck, G.C. & Kupecky, R.M. (1995). (See above)

9. Henderson, A.T., Dahlin, I, Partridge, C.R., & Engelsing, E.L. (1973). A hypothesis on the etiology of hyperactivity, with a pilot study report of related nondrug therapy. *Pediatrics*, Vol. 52, no. 4, p. 625.

Vorstr, de Wet. (1990). "Holding" as a therapeutic manoeuvre in family therapy. *Journal of Family Therapy*, Vol. 12, no. 2, 189-194.

10. Diagnostic and Statistical Manual of Mental Disorders, Edition IV. (1994). American Psychiatric Association.

11. Fischer, M. (1990). Parenting stress and the child with attention deficit hyperactivity disorder. *Journal of Clinical Child Psychology*, Vol. 19, no. 4, 337-346.

Bower, B. (1988). Hyperactivity: The Family Factor. *Science News,* June 18, p. 399.

Safer, D.A. (1973). A familial factor in minimal brain dysfunction. *Behavior Genetics*, 3, 175-186.

12. Van der Kolk, B.A. (1987). *Psychological Trauma*. Washington, DC: American Psychiatric Press.

Stevens, J., Sachdev, K., & Milstein, V. (1968). Behavior disorders of childhood and the electroencephalogram. *Archives of Neurology*, 18, 160-177.

Jacobvitz, D. & Sroufe, L. (1987). The early caregiver-child relationship and attention-deficit disorder with hyperactivity in kindergarten: A prospective study. *Child Development*, 58, 1496-1504.

13. National Institute of Health Publication No. 94-3572 (1994): *Attention Deficit Hyperactivity Disorder*.

14. Welch, M. *Holding Time*. (1988). New York: Simon and Schuster.

15. Armstrong, T. (1995). *The Myth of the A.D.D. Child: Fifty ways to improve your child's behavior and attention span without labels, drugs, or coercion*. Dutton.

16. Van der Kolk, B.A. (1987) (See above)

6. ADULT MEMORIES OF CRYING AS CHILDREN: HOW CRYING IS REPRESSED (no references cited)

7. DIFFERENCES IN CRYING BETWEEN MEN AND WOMEN (page 37)

1. Hastrup, J, Kraemer, D., Bornstein, R. (1985). Crying frequency of 1- to 12-year-old boys and girls. Paper presented at the annual meeting of the Eastern Psychological Association, Boston, March 1985. (Quoted in Frey, 1985).

2. Kottler, J.A. (1996). *The Language of Tears*. San Francisco: Jossey-Bass, Inc.

3. Askew, S. & Ross, C. (1988). *Boys Don't Cry: Boys and Sexism in Education*. Philadelphia: Open University Press.

   Beal, C. (1994). *Boys and Girls: The Development of Gender Roles*. New York: McGraw-Hill.

   Miedzian, M. (1991). *Boys Will be Boys: Breaking the Link Between Masculinity and Violence*. New York: Doubleday.

   Silverstein, O. & Rashbaum, B. (1994). *The Courage to Raise Good Men*. New York: Viking.

4. Frey, II, W.H. & Langseth, M. (1985). *Crying: The Mystery of Tears*. Winston Press.

5. Hales, D. (1981). Psycho-immunity. *Science Digest*. (Nov.),12-14.

6. Carmen, E.H., Reiker, P.P., Mills, T. (1984). Victims of violence and psychiatric illness. *American Journal of Psychiatry*, 141: 378-379.

8. CONTROL PATTERNS IN ADULTS (no references cited)

PART II: CRYING IN INFANTS

1. EXPLANATIONS FOR CRYING DURING INFANCY (pages 43 to 46)

1. Brazelton, T.B. (1962). Crying in infancy. *Pediatrics*, 29, 579-588.
2. Barr, R., Konner, M., Bakeman, R., and Adamson, L. (1991). Crying in !Kung infants: A test of the cultural specificity hypothesis. *Developmental Medicine and Child Neurology*, 33, 601-610.
3. Spock, B. (1992). *Dr. Spock's Baby and Child Care*. New York: Pocket Books.
4. Jorup, S. (1982). Colonic hyperperistalsis in neurolabile infants. *Acta Pediatrica Uppsala*, Supplement 85, 1-92.
   Wessel, M.A. (1965). Paroxysmal fussing in infancy, sometimes called "colic." *Pediatrics*, 14, 421-434.
5. Kirkland, J. (1985). *Crying and Babies: Helping Families Cope*. Dover, NH: Croom Helm Ltd.
6. Sears, W. & Sears, M. (1993). *The Baby Book: Everything you Need to Know About Your Baby From Birth to Age Two*. Little, Brown & Company.
7. Barr, R., Adelson, J., Tanser, C., and Wooldridge, J. (1987). Effect of formula protein change on crying behavior. *Pediatric Research*, 21, A179.
8. Jakobsson, I. & Lindberg, T. (1983). Cow's milk proteins cause infantile colic in breast-fed infants: a double-blind crossover study. *Pediatrics*, 71, 268-271.
9. Solter, A. (1984). *The Aware Baby: A New Approach to Parenting*. Goleta, CA: Shining Star Press.
10. deZegher, F., Vanhole, C., Van den Berghe, G., Devlieger, H., Eggermont, E., Veldhuis, J.D. (1994). Properties of thyroid-stimulating hormone and cortisol secretion by the human newborn on the day of birth. *Journal of Clinical Endocrinology and Metabolism*, 79(2), 576-581.
11. Lewis, M. & Ramsay, D. (1995). Stability and change in cortisol and behavioral response to stress during the first 18 months of life. *Developmental Psychobiology*, 28(8) 419-428.
12. Gunnar, M.R., Mangelsdorf, S., Larson, M., & Hertsgaard, L. (1989). Attachment, temperament, and adrenocortical activity in infancy: A study of psycho-endocrine regulation. *Developmental Psychology*, 25, 355-363.

2. SOURCES OF STRESS FOR INFANTS (pages 47 to 54)

1. Verny, T. (1981). *The Secret Life of the Unborn Child*. New York: Dell.
   Chamberlain, D.B. (1992). Is there intelligence before birth? *Pre- and Perinatal Psychology Journal*, 6(3), 217-237.
2. Kizinger, S. (1989). *The Crying Baby*. Viking.
3. Janov, A. (1983). *Imprints: The Lifelong Effects of the Birth Experience*. New York: Coward-McCann, Inc.
4. Emerson, W.R. (1987). Psychotherapy with infants. *Pre- and Perinatal Psychology News*, 1(2).
5. Kitzinger, S. (1989). (See above)
6. Bernal, J.F. (1973). Night waking in infants during the first 14 months. *Developmental Medicine and Child Neurology*, 15(6), 760-769.
7. Murray, A.D., Dolby, R.M., Nation, R.L., & Thomas, D.B. (1981). Effects of epidural anesthesia on newborns and their mothers. *Child Development*, 52, 71-82.
8. Hunziker, V.A. and Barr, R.G. (1986). Increased carrying reduces infant crying: A randomized controlled trial. *Pediatrics*, 77, 641-648.
9. Glantz, K. & Pearce, J. (1989). *Exiles From Eden*. New York: W.W. Norton & Company.
10. Thevenin, T. (1976). *The Family Bed: An Age Old Concept in Childrearing*. Thevenin, T. P.O. Box 16004, Minneapolis, MN.
    Liedloff, J. (1975). *The Continuum Concept*. Addison-Wesley Publishing Company, Inc.
    Solter, A. (1984). *The Aware Baby: A New Approach to Parenting*. Goleta, CA: Shining Star Press.
    Sears, W. & Sears, M. (1993). *The Baby Book: Everything you Need to Know About Your Baby From Birth to Age Two*. Little, Brown & Company.
11. Barnard, K.E. (1973). The effects of stimulation on the sleep behaviors of the premature infant. In M. Batty (Ed.). *Western Journal for Communicating Nursing Research*, Vol. 6.
12. Brazelton, T.B. (1985). Application of cry research to clinical perspectives. In B.M. Lester and C.F.Z. Boukydis (Eds.). *Infant Crying: Theoretical and Research Perspectives*. New York: Plenum Press.
13. Lester, B.M. & Boukydis, C.F. (1985). *Infant Crying: Theoretical and Research Perspectives*. New York: Plenum Press.
14. Lewis, M. & Ramsay, D.S. (1995). Developmental changes in infants' responses to stress. *Child Development*, 66(3), 657-670.

Rosendahl, W., Schulz, U., Teufel, T., Irtel von Brenndorf, C., & Gupta, D. (1995). Surgical stress and neuroendocrine responses in infants and children. Journal of Pediatric Endocrinology and Metabolism, 8(3), 187-194.
15. Gunnar, M.R., Larson, M.C., Hertsgaard, L., Harris, M.L., & Brodersen, L. (1992). The stressfulness of separation among nine-month-old infants: effects of social context variables and infant temperament. *Child Development*, 63, 290-303.

3. WHAT TO DO WHEN BABIES CRY (no references cited)

4. HOW TO REDUCE STRESS AND THE NEED FOR CRYING DURING INFANCY (pages 61 to 63)

1. Frey, II, W.H. & Langseth, M. (1985). *Crying: The Mystery of Tears.* Winston Press.

5. HOW CRYING IS REPRESSED IN BABIES: THE ORIGIN OF CONTROL PATTERNS (pages 64 to 74)

1. Konner, M.J. (1972). Aspects of the developmental ethology of a foraging people. In N. Blurton Jones (Ed.), *Ethological Studies of Child Behavior*. Cambridge: Cambridge University Press, 1972.
2. Shostak, M. (1981). *Nisa: The Life and Words of a !Kung Woman*. New York: Vintage Books.
3. deMause, L. (1974). *The History of Childhood*. The Psychohistory Press.
4. Fagot, B.I., and Kronsberg, S.J. (1982). Sex differences: biological and social factors influencing the behavior of young boys and girls. In S.G. Moore and C.R. Cooper (Eds.). *The Young Child: Reviews of Research* (Vol. 3). National Association for the Education of Young Children, Washington, DC.
5. Konner, M.J.(1972). (See above)
6. Mayr, D. F. & Boelderl, A. R. (1993). The Pacifier Craze: Collective Regression in Europe. *The Journal of Psychohistory*, 21 (2), 143-156.
7. Kitzinger, S. (1985). *The Crying Baby*. Viking.
8. Armstrong, T. (1995). *The Myth of the A.D.D. Child*. Dutton.
9. Mayr, D.F. & Beolderl, A.R. (1993). (See above)
10. Kitzinger, S. (1985). (See above)

6. HELPING BABIES SLEEP THROUGH THE NIGHT (WITHOUT IGNORING THEM) (pages 75 to 78)

1. Kirkland, J. (1985). *Crying and Babies: Helping Families Cope.* London & Dover, NH: Croom Helm, Ltd.
2. Solter, A. (1984). *The Aware Baby: A New Approach to Parenting..* Goleta, CA: Shining Star Press.

PART III: CRYING AND RAGING IN CHILDREN

1. SOURCES OF STRESS FOR CHILDREN (pages 81 to 82)

1. Solter, A. (1984). *The Aware Baby: A New Approach to Parenting.* Goleta, CA: Shining Star Press.
   Solter, A. (1989). *Helping Young Children Flourish.* Goleta, CA: Shining Star Press.
2. Gordon, T. (1975). *Parent Effectiveness Training.* New York: New American Library.
3. Elkind, D. (1981). *The Hurried Child: Growing up Too Fast Too Soon.* Addison-Wesley.

2. WHAT TO DO WHEN CHILDREN CRY (pages 83 to 84)

1. Gordon, T. (1975). *Parent Effectiveness Training.* New York: New American Library.

3. THE "BROKEN COOKIE" PHENOMENON (pages 85 to 88)

1. Wipfler, P. (1989). *Listening: A Tool for Powerful Parenting.* The Parents Leadership Institute (P.O. Box 50492, Palo Alto, CA 94303.
   Solter, A. (1989). Helping Young Children Flourish. Goleta, CA: Shining Star Press.

4. DEALING WITH PHYSICAL HURTS (pages 89 to 90)

1. Cioffi, D. & Holloway, J. (1993). Delayed costs of suppressed pain. *Journal of Personality and Social Psychology,* 64(2), 274-282.

5. CRYING DURING SEPARATIONS (pages 91 to 96)

1. Ainsworth, M.D.S. (1977). Social development in the first year of life: maternal influences on infant-mother attachment. In J.M. Tanner (Ed.). *Developments in Psychiatric Research*. London: Tavistock.

6. DEALING WITH VIOLENCE (pages 97 to 103)

1. Miedzian, M. (1991). *Boys Will be Boys: Breaking the link Between Masculinity and Violence*. Doubleday.
2. Löfgren, L.B. (1966). On Weeping. *International Journal of Psycho-Analysis*, 47, 375-381.
3. Stone, J.G.S. (1969). *A Guide to Discipline*. Washington, DC: National Association for the Education of Young Children.

7. BEDTIME CRYING (pages 104 to 105)

1. Bowlby, J. (1988). *A Secure Base*. Basic Books, Inc.
2. Frank, A. (1952). *Anne Frank: The Diary of a Young Girl*. New York: Simon and Schuster, Inc.

8. HELPING CHILDREN HEAL FROM SPECIFIC TRAUMATIC EVENTS (pages 106 to 109)

1. Sullivan, M.A., Saylor, C.F., & Foster, K.Y. (1991). Post-hurricane adjustment of preschoolers and their families. *Advances in Behavior Research and Therapy*, 13, 163-171.
2. Udwin, O. (1993). Children's reactions to traumatic events. *Journal of Child Psychology and Psychiatry*, Vol. 34, 115-127.

PART IV: PRACTICAL APPLICATIONS

1. INTERPRETING CHILDREN'S BEHAVIOR (no references cited)

2. CREATING EMOTIONAL SAFETY (pages 115 to 118)

1. Solter, A. (1984). *The Aware Baby*. Goleta, CA: Shining Star Press.
   Solter, A. (1989). *Helping Young Children Flourish*. Goleta, CA: Shining Star Press.
   Gordon, T. (1975). *Parent Effectiveness Training*. New York: New American Library.
2. Gordon, T. (1975). (See above)

3. DEALING WITH YOUR OWN FEELINGS (pages 119 to 122)

1. Fraiberg, S. (1980). *Clinical Studies in Infant Mental Health*. New York: Basic Books.

4. PARENTS SHARE THEIR EXPERIENCES (no references cited)

5. THE MOST COMMONLY ASKED QUESTIONS (pages 134 to 148)

1. Solter, A. (1989). *Helping Young Children Flourish*. Goleta, CA: Shining Star Press.
   Solter, A. (1992). The Disadvantages of Time-Out. *Mothering*. (No. 65)
   Solter, A. (1994). Time-Out: should you or shouldn't you? *Parenting* (October).
2. Glantz, K. & Pearce, J. (1989). *Exiles From Eden*. New York: W.W. Norton & Company.
3. Ostwald, P.F. & Murry, T. (1985). The communicative and diagnostic significance of infant sounds. In B.M. Lester and C.F.Z. Boukydis (Eds.). *Infant Crying: Theoretical and Research Perspectives*. New York: Plenum Press.

6. SUPPORTING PARENTS OF CHILDREN WHO CRY (no references cited)

SUGGESTIONS FOR FURTHER READING

If you wish to explore further the ideas presented in this book, the following books, pamphlets, and journals contain information about crying and listening to children.

The Aware Baby by Aletha Solter, Ph.D. (1984). This is the author's first book, originally published in 1984, representing a breakthrough in our understanding of babies' emotional needs. It describes in detail how to parent a baby from birth to two-and-a-half years of age while recognizing and accepting the need to cry. Translated into German, French, Dutch, and Italian. (English language edition available from Shining Star Press, P.O. Box 206, Goleta, California 93116. See order form at back of book.)

Helping Young Children Flourish, by Aletha Solter, Ph.D. (1989). The author's second book is a sequel to *The Aware Baby*, and continues this same approach with children from two to eight years of age. Translated into German and French. (English language edition available from Shining Star Press, P.O. Box 206, Goleta, California 93116. See order form at back of book.)

Parent Effectiveness Training, by Thomas Gordon, Ph.D. (1975). This important book describes the basic principles of active listening, I-messages, and non-punitive conflict-resolution. A classic that all parents should read. Other recommended books by Thomas Gordon are *Teacher Effectiveness Training* and *Teaching Children Self-Discipline*. There is also a home video program in Parent Effectiveness Training. (Gordon Training International, 531 Stevens Ave. West, Solana Beach, California 92075. 1-800-628-1197 or 1-619-481-8121.)

Crying: the Mystery of Tears, by William Frey II, Ph.D. & M. Langseth (1985). Dr. Frey, a biochemist, describes the methods, results, and conclusions of his studies on tears and crying. Does not require prior knowledge of biochemistry. (Winston Press.)

The Crying Baby by Sheila Kitzinger (1989). This book cites many interesting research studies about crying during infancy. (Viking Press.)

Helping Children Cope With Separation and Loss by Claudia L. Jewett (1982). The author describes the feelings of grieving children, and offers concrete suggestions for helping them work through their grief. (Harvard Common Press.)

Holding Time, by Martha Welch, M.D. (1988). Psychiatrist Welch describes how parents can use a holding technique effectively with their children to re-establish a strong bond. The therapeutic holding she describes often involves crying and raging. (Simon and Schuster.)

The Wildest Colts Make the Best Horses, by John Breeding, Ph.D. (1996). The subtitle of this book is: "The truth about Ritalin, A.D.H.D. and other Disruptive Behavior Disorders." Alternatives to drug therapy for children with attention disorders or hyperactivity, including an approach based on releasing pent-up, painful emotions through crying and raging. (Bright Books, Inc. Available from John Breeding, 2503 Douglas Street, Austin, Texas 78741.)

Listening to Children (set of 6 pamphlets) by Patty Wipfler. These pamphlets describe a respectful, listening approach for children's various forms of emotional release. (The Parents Leadership Institute, P.O. Box 50492, Palo Alto, California 94303.)

Our Children Ourselves, edited by Pamela Haines. A bi-yearly journal by and for parents about raising children with respect and allowing them to release painful emotions. Back issues available. (Our Children Ourselves, 919 S. Farragut Street, Philadelphia, Pennsylvania 19143.)

Index

ABOUT THE AUTHOR

Aletha Solter, Ph.D., is a Swiss/American developmental psychologist, international speaker, workshop leader, consultant, and the mother of two children. She studied with the Swiss psychologist, Dr. Jean Piaget, at the University of Geneva, Switzerland, where she obtained a Master's degree in human biology. She holds a Ph.D. in psychology from the University of California at Santa Barbara. Her two previous books, *The Aware Baby* (birth to 2° years) and *Helping Young Children Flourish* (2 to 8 years) have been translated into several languages. She has also written workbooks to accompany these two books, as well as numerous articles for parents and educators.

Since 1978, she has been working with parents and professionals involved with children, and she has led workshops in eight countries. In 1990 she founded the Aware Parenting Institute to promote the philosophy of child-rearing based on her work. "Aware Parenting" combines attachment-style parenting, non-punitive discipline, and acceptance of emotional release. There is a growing list of certified Aware Parenting instructors.

Dr. Solter lives in Goleta, California, and can be reached at the address below. She is available for private consultations, talks, and workshops.

The Aware Parenting Institute
P.O. Box 206
Goleta, California 93116
U.S.A.

Phone & Fax: (805) 968-1868
e-mail: awarepar@sb.net
web site: http://www.sb.net/awarepar/

OTHER BOOKS BY ALETHA SOLTER, Ph.D.

(See order form on page 177)

The Aware Baby: A new approach to parenting
(birth to two-and-a-half years, 276 pages)

This revolutionary book, now translated into German, French, Dutch, and Italian, marks a major breakthrough in our understanding of babies' emotional needs. The author questions most of the traditional beliefs about babies, and proposes an approach to parenting based on respect and trust. At the core of her philosophy is the concept of emotional release, specifically the healing power of crying while being lovingly held and listened to. The topics covered include birth and bonding, early needs, crying, sleep problems, feeding issues, play, stimulation and learning, alternatives to punishments and rewards, toddler interactions, toilet training, and attachment issues.

"I have recommended this book to thousands of parents and professionals, with outstanding results."
-William R. Emerson, Ph.D., Pioneer in infant and child psychotherapy

Helping Young Children Flourish
(two to eight years, 245 pages)

As a sequel to *The Aware Baby*, this book continues the same approach, focusing on the development and emotional needs of children up to eight years of age. Now translated into German and French, this book provides much useful advice for coping with day-to-day problems, as well as guidelines for helping children reach their full potential. The topics covered include crying and raging, violent behavior, fears, stimulation and learning, play and fantasy, bedtime problems, alternatives to punishments and rewards, siblings and peer relationships, eating issues, hospitalization, bedwetting, and hyperactivity.

"It is a fine book, full of sound ideas to make parenting easier and to help children flourish."
-Thomas Gordon, Ph.D., Founder, Gordon Training International

Workbooks:

The Aware Baby Workbook
Helping Young Children Flourish Workbook
(40 pages each, large format)

These practical guides to accompany *The Aware Baby* and *Helping Young Children Flourish* are based on Aletha Solter's classes and workshops. They are packed with a great variety of exercises that have proven to be useful and enjoyable for parents of babies and young children. These workbooks also outline the key concepts of each chapter by means of summary charts, handy for quick reference. They can be used alone, with a partner, or in a group setting.

Parents are encouraged to form Aware Parenting Support Groups in order to discuss these concepts with other parents, share experiences and feelings, and give each other support. These workbooks can serve as a complete guide for group activities.

ORDER FORM

To order Aletha Solter's books or workbooks, please fill out this form and send it with your payment (U.S. check or international money order) to Shining Star Press, P.O. Box 206, Goleta, California 93116, U.S.A.

Shipping fees for inside the U.S.: Book rate: add $1.50 to your order for the first book, 50¢ for each additional book. Allow up to 30 days for delivery. For priority mail: add $3.00 per book.

Shipping fees for outside the U.S.: International book rate for all countries (surface mail): add $2.00 to your order for the first book, $1.00 for each additional book. Allow 30 to 90 days for delivery. Airmail to other countries: add the following amount per book: Canada & Mexico: $4.00, Central & South America: $6.00, Europe: $8.00, Asia & Africa: $9.00, Pacific Rim: $10.00.

Please inquire about our discount rates for bulk orders.
Phone & fax: (805) 968-1868, e-mail: awarepar@sb.net

- -

Number
of copies:

_____ *Tears and Tantrums* ($12.95)...$_____

_____ *The Aware Baby* ($11.95)...$_____

_____ *Helping Young Children Flourish* ($11.95).......................$_____

_____ *The Aware Baby Workbook* ($8.00)...................................$_____

_____ *Helping Young Children Flourish Workbook* ($8.00).....$_____

Subtotal...$_____

Sales tax (California residents only)..................................$_____

Shipping fee (see above)...$_____

Total amount enclosed...$_____

Name and address (please print):

_____

_____

_____

_____